Opening the Book of Faith

Lutheran Insights for Bible Study

Diane Jacobson

Stanley N. Olson

Mark Allan Powell

Trinity Lutheran Seminary

Augsburg Fortress

MINNEAPOLIS

OPENING THE BOOK OF FAITH
Lutheran Insights for Bible Study

This book is accompanied by a downloadable Leader Guide (ISBN 978-0806680583).

 Book of Faith is an initiative of the
Evangelical Lutheran Church in America.

Scripture quotations, unless otherwise marked, are from the New Revised Standard Version Bible, copyright © 1989 by the Division of Christian Education of the National Council of Churches of Christ in the USA. Used by permission. All rights reserved.

Bible Study Writers: Diane Jacobson, Paul Lutz, Kathryn Kleinhans, R. Guy Erwin
Book of Faith Assessment Tools: Norma Cook Everist
Editor: Scott Tunseth
Cover and interior design: Spunk Design Machine, spkdm.com

Library of Congress Cataloging-in-Publication Data
Jacobson, Diane L., 1948–
  Opening the Book of Faith : Lutheran insights for Bible study / Diane L. Jacobson, Stanley N. Olson.
    p. cm.
  Includes bibliographical references.
  ISBN 978-0-8066-8056-9 (alk. paper)
  1. Bible--Study and teaching. 2. Bible--Study and teaching--Lutheran Church.
  3. Lutheran Church--Doctrines. I. Powell, Mark Allan, 1953- II. Title.
  BS600.3.J33 2008
  220.071--dc22   2008016621

13   12   11   10   09   3   4   5   6   7   8   9   10   11

Contents

Preface   vii

1. God's Powerful Book   1

2. How Can Lutheran Insights Open Up the Bible?   20

3. How Can the Bible Be Studied?   46

4. Four Bible Studies   66
   Study 1: Exodus 3:1-15   68
   Study 2: Jeremiah 1:4-19   78
   Study 3: John 8:31-36   85
   Study 4: Romans 7:15-25a   92

Endnotes   100

Book of Faith Assessment Tools   104

Preface

In 2007 the ELCA churchwide assembly voted to embrace an initiative called Book of Faith. The bold vision for this five-year initiative is:

> That the whole church become more fluent in the first language of faith, the language of Scripture, in order that we might live into our calling as a people renewed, enlivened, empowered, and sent by the Word.

This book, *Opening the Book of Faith*, is your invitation to engage in this vision. Through this book and through this initiative, we will be called to experience more fully the power of the Word and to recall or learn anew the Lutheran approaches to Scripture that have been so fruitful over the centuries.

In chapter 1, Stan Olson explores how Lutherans think of God's powerful Word and why we talk of the Bible as a Book of Faith. In chapter 2, Mark Allan Powell introduces how Lutheran insights help us open up the Bible. In chapter 3, you will be introduced to four approaches to studying the Bible that can be used in concert to deepen and broaden your experience in Bible study. You are then invited to experience the power of studying biblical texts together through four group Bible studies.

The Book of Faith initiative calls for a conversation that is deep and broad, including folks of all ages and across all the many cultures that inform who we are as a people of God. To help you in your local setting, we have also included in this book two tools to help you assess engagement with the Bible in your congregation or organization. To learn more about these tools, the Book of Faith initiative, and the various ways you can join the conversation and live out the vision, visit our Web site (www.elca.org/bookoffaith).

The Book of Faith initiative envisions a church renewed and empowered for faithful service. This renewal can be fueled by groups coming together and exploring the Bible in depth. As we open Scripture and faithfully join in conversation, the Bible will come alive for us anew. With God's help we will discover new ways to hear and share God's living Word. God's Spirit will help us express more fluently the biblical message and the unique Lutheran insights that define who we are as God's people. God will open us—individually and as communities of faith—to the gospel, which the Apostle Paul declares, "is the power of God for salvation to everyone who has faith" (Romans 1:16).

So . . . let's get started! Open Scripture. Join the Conversation.

Diane Jacobson, Director of the Book of Faith initiative of the ELCA

For more information on how to use this book in a group setting, go to augsburgfortress.org/bookoffaith.

1. God's Powerful Book

Stanley N. Olson

For as the rain and the snow come down from heaven,
    and do not return there until they have watered the earth,
making it bring forth and sprout,
    giving seed to the sower and bread to the eater,
so shall my word be that goes out from my mouth;
    it shall not return to me empty,
but it shall accomplish that which I purpose,
    and succeed in the thing for which I sent it.
    —Isaiah 55.10-11

Heaven and earth will pass away, but my words will not pass away
    —Mark 13:31

The Bible is astonishingly powerful. The Bible changes this sin-filled world. Through the Bible, God engages us with demands that judge us. Through it God engages us with promise, forgiveness, and hope, setting us free to love and serve. Through the Bible, God draws us to trust, to faith in the good news of Jesus Christ. Through the Bible, the Spirit of God calls, gathers, enlightens and makes holy the entire people of God.

Statistical, external evidence reveals the powerful influence of the Bible even in our modern world. It is a perennial best seller. All forms of communications media are used to share biblical texts. Every Christian church building has Bibles in abundance. Even in the face of poverty, a Christian home has a Bible. The Bible's impact on culture, literature, and law is broad and deep.

Far more importantly, the practices of Christians demonstrate that the Bible is powerful. Because we are so accustomed to the Bible being read in worship and used as the basis for the sermons, we may fail to consider how amazing it is that this ancient book still gets such attention. Individuals read and study the book because they know it engages them, for good. By policy and in practice, congregations, church bodies, and affiliated institutions turn to the Scriptures for direction. Polls show that Americans in general and Lutherans in particular claim to read the Bible regularly.

An Authoritative Word

Lutherans say that the Bible has authority. In doing so, we confess faith in the God who engages us there. We worship a living, active, relevant God who continues in relationship with creation, with humanity, with the church, with each of us. Through the Bible, God engages us. God speaks to each of us, with challenge and with promise. That's the Bible's authority.

So, when we speak of the *authority* of the Bible, we claim a promise. Lutherans say the Bible is *inspired*. The Spirit of God speaks there. This is bold expectation. We are confident that through the Bible, God will address us in our contemporary realities, just as God has addressed humanity over the centuries. We praise God by this confidence, gratefully astonished that God engages us through the Bible.

To say a written text is authoritative might mean several things. For example, a text might be authoritative because concepts articulated there are generally accepted. An official rule book for some sport or game has this sort of authority. Or, a text may be considered authoritative because it is the best available account of an event, a life, a location, or a phenomenon. Histories, biographies, travel guides, and scientific articles can have such authority. For Lutherans, the Bible includes such authoritative elements, but its effective authority has another source.

The Bible is authoritative because it communicates the grace of God in Jesus Christ. It commuicates to us as law and gospel, demand and promise. The Bible is authoritative for us because it allows us to encounter the gracious God who was self-revealed in Jesus of Nazareth. In fact, the Bible is authoritative for us in much the same way that Jesus Christ was authoritative for those first-century women and men who became his disciples. They encountered God in him. We encounter God through the Bible because it effectively conveys Jesus Christ to us. One Lutheran scholar from the 1930s describes this central focus on Jesus in this way: "We must state anew our

Lutheran attitude toward the Scriptures from the Christocentric point of view. The Scriptures are more than the historical record of God's revelation in Christ. The Word of God has a center, Christ Himself."[1] God in Jesus Christ engages people through the Bible. The book is a means of grace.

Therefore, and this is a very important "therefore," Lutherans begin with what the Bible *does*, rather than beginning with claims about its nature or origin. Lutherans do not think that one must trust the Bible in order to make faith possible. Rather, we know that the Bible creates faith in those who hear it. So, to enable people to believe, we invite them into the faith community to listen with us to God speaking through the Bible and through proclamation. We confidently anticipate that God's Spirit will nurture trust in those who read and hear the Bible. Our Lutheran customs demonstrate this confidence.

For example, people are not asked to declare their belief in the Bible in important rites such as Baptism or Confirmation, or even when they become new members. Rather, they are asked to be engaged by the Bible. Lutherans do not attempt to *prove* that the Bible is inspired by God or authoritative. Rather, we testify to what we and other believers have experienced: The Bible is powerful because God addresses us there with demand and promise. It is authoritative for us. It changes lives. As one Lutheran teacher puts it, ". . . the authority of scripture rests on that of the gospel and its content—the saving presence of God in the person and history of Jesus Christ. . . . The church endorses the Bible only for the sake of the gospel, and the gospel only for the sake of the reconciliation of the world by God in the death of Jesus Christ. . . ."[2]

When Lutherans talk about biblical authority, they say that the Bible's power has its source in God through Jesus Christ, and that this power is known through God's Spirit. The power does not belong to the book itself. The Bible is powerful—full of God's power, as Christ is. This power is not detached from God and left behind in the words on the page. God's voice there is living. On the other hand, though the Bible's power is seen in its impact on the hearer who experiences demand and promise, the power is not dependent upon the hearer. The authority of the Bible comes from God.

Authority is not bestowed on the Bible by those who believe. When we speak of the authority of Scripture, we mean that God powerfully addresses us there.

The Book of Faith

> So faith comes from what is heard, and what is heard comes through the word of Christ.
> —*Romans 10:17*

To be engaged by God is to be made a person of faith, trusting God who is revealed in Jesus Christ. The Bible's authority is shown when God creates faith, through demand and promise. We do trust the Bible. However, our trust of the book depends upon our trust in God, the Father, Son, and Holy Spirit. The Bible is a means by which God communicates grace, through Jesus Christ. The Bible nurtures faith.

The Bible also comes from faith. God used faithful people to remember and reveal God's engagement with humanity, from the beginning. People of faith eventually wrote down the stories, poetry, prophesies, insights, and discussions that came from God's engagement with people. The parts of the Bible and eventually the whole of it were preserved and used by people of faith. God created that faith too.

And, the Bible is a book of faith because we are invited to come to it in faith—faith in God who saves us through Christ and faith that God will engage us and all people through these texts. When we open the Scripture, we join a conversation in faith, a conversation that God's powerful book sustains. And the very faith with which we approach the texts is also God's creation.

The Bible is God's powerful book of faith—for faith, from faith, in faith. The Bible is called "holy" because it is set apart by God for humanity in order to convey Christ and nurture faith.

God's Powerful Word

> And God said, "Let there be. . .and it was so and God saw everything
> that he had made, and indeed, it was very good.
> —*Genesis 1:3, 30-31*

> In the beginning was the Word and the Word was with God, and the
> Word was God. . . . And the Word became flesh and lived among us. . . .
> —*John 1:1, 14*

God speaks in Jesus the Christ.
God speaks through the believers telling the story of God's love in Jesus Christ.
God speaks through the Bible.

These three convictions are parts of one truth. Together they declare the foundation of faith.

God speaks. Lutherans are so familiar with this claim that we may miss its audacity. We are confident that God speaks. We hear this assumption in texts read in worship and in the assumption that texts should be read in worship. We hear it in sermons and in the assumption that worship should include sermons. It is articulated in familiar liturgical responses, such as "This is the Word of the Lord," and in ordinary conversation among Christians: "I was reading the Psalms today, and God really spoke to me." Or, "Pastor, God spoke to me through your sermon today." In all such practices and language, Lutherans are showing confidence in a God who is not absent, distant, or uninvolved. God is present in the speaking of God's Word.

The Bible itself continually portrays God as speaking—directly, through prophets, apostles, leaders, and poets, in Jesus of Nazareth, in the texts of Scripture. The Bible assumes that God addresses people.

The Confession of Faith of the Evangelical Lutheran Church in America carefully affirms and illuminates three aspects of God's powerful speaking:

2.02. This church confesses Jesus Christ as Lord and Savior and the Gospel
as the power of God for the salvation of all who believe.

God speaks to us through:

Jesus Christ

a. Jesus Christ is the Word of God incarnate, through whom everything was made and through whose life, death, and resurrection God fashions a new creation.

Preach of the Word

b. The proclamation of God's message to us as both Law and Gospel is the Word of God, revealing judgment and mercy through word and deed, beginning with the Word in creation, continuing in the history of Israel, and centering in all its fullness in the person and work of Jesus Christ.

Scripture

c. The canonical Scriptures of the Old and New Testaments are the written Word of God. Inspired by God's Spirit speaking through their authors, they record and announce God's revelation centering in Jesus Christ. Through them God's Spirit speaks to us to create and sustain Christian faith and fellowship for service in the world.[3]

These constitutional paragraphs are first of all a testimony to truth. The words describe the three-fold Christian experience of being addressed by God—through Jesus Christ, through the speaking of other believers, and through the text of Bible. This language also shows the church's commitment to hear the Bible so that we can hear God speaking. Further, these paragraphs assert that individual members of the church will be expectant listeners. And, finally, these constitutional words are also an evangelical invitation to anyone: "Listen with us."

Note in the constitutional language that the introductory statement and each of the three expansive clauses refers to Jesus Christ. Lutherans are convinced that Jesus Christ is the definitive Word of God and that the Bible's primary function is to convey Christ.

This section of the ELCA Confession of Faith begins with reference to "the salvation of all who believe," and ends with ". . . service in the world." We believe that the Word of God is for everyone. The Bible is intended for the good of all, directly through God's engagement and indirectly through the service of those who have been engaged by God.

Lutherans believe that the Word of God through the Bible is for each person in his or her own life, but our confidence for individuals is inseparable from the conviction that the Bible is an inherited and shared gift. The

Bible is given to the whole of Christ's church. We received this gift from those who were part of Christ's church before us, and we hear the Bible now in the company of all others who look to it as authoritative.

These statements are prominent in the constitutional Confession of Faith of the ELCA because the belief is essential to our identity as a church. When one says, "Lutherans read the Bible," it might be merely a description, and some might dispute its statistical accuracy. However, "Lutherans read the Bible" is a statement of self-understanding. Even when we fail to act upon it, we know it is true. The Bible is where God speaks, so we have no identity without it. We are individuals, congregations, synods, ministries, and institutions of the Bible. We share this confession with all Lutherans.

The Bible is authoritative because God speaks there. That means that humans are not in control of God's message for our lives of faith, individually and as the church. God fully engages us, with our intellects and our experience and our contexts, but it is God who speaks, and we are not in control. This *Opening the Book of Faith* volume talks about and demonstrates Lutheran insights and methods for Bible study. Lutherans will put their best thinking and hard work into the study of the Bible, but they always intend to acknowledge God's voice through their insights and methods. Lutherans aim to be attentive listeners, hearing God's living word for this church, our lives, these days.

The Word of God does not simply convey information; it engages us. This reality and how it works can be described in various ways. One useful image is that God's Word creates a world into which we are invited.[4] God welcomes us to and helps us inhabit this world of proclaimed law and gospel. It is in this world that we die to all that is alien to God and are made alive by the promise inherent in God's speaking to us. Put another way, God's Word is like a lens that helps us see the world and our life in a real way. Through engagement with the Bible, we recognize our fears and failures, but that is only part of the reality. Because of the good news of the gospel, we also see and experience forgiveness and joy and hope.

With great effectiveness for more than two thousand years, the Bible has projected this vision of God's reality, and a continuing community has found its identity there. The Bible's vision includes a gracious and righteous God to whom thankful obedience is due. The Bible reveals God who is known most truly in the life, death, and resurrection of Jesus, who is powerfully present in everyday life, and who frees people from the deathward pull of rebellious self-centeredness. We live in this world of the Bible.

Another image is that the Word becomes our food and drink. The prophet "Ezekiel, during his call to become a prophet, was handed a written scroll and commanded to eat it. . . . (Ezek 3:1) The episode provides a vivid image of how the Scriptures are to be internalized, influencing every fiber of a person's being and identity."[5] The voice of God's wisdom in Isaiah 55 uses the same image—Come, eat and drink! The Word of God becomes vital to our lives. We need continually to receive it into ourselves where it feeds us.

Fluency is a particularly useful image for a church convinced that God speaks. God's engagement with us is so complete that the language of God's self revelation becomes our own. The Bible teaches us our mother tongue. We learn and practice that language in liturgy, creeds, symbols, songs, hymns, and daily talk.

> We need to remember that all forms of the mother tongue for faith go back to one matrix ("matrix" is a Latin word derived from *mater*, "mother"): the mother soil is Scripture. . . . Scripture as the common matrix, the mother soil of all forms of the Christian mother tongue—might this be the answer to the search of experiential faith for its language?[6]

We desire to accept God's offer of fluency in our mother tongue so that we can hear clearly the words of demand and promise that give us life and so that we can praise God faithfully for the gift we have experienced and can share it. Fluency comes from knowing the Bible well, but begins simply with hearing Christian proclamation, and grows by grace. God allows us to take God-bearing words on our lips. Pastors and other public ministers of the Word speak these words on behalf of us all. And each of us speaks these words and conveys grace as we talk with others— parent to child, neighbor to neighbor, worker to worker, friend to friend. As Luther said, we are Christ to one another.

A Bible-Shaped People

> Go therefore and make disciples of all nations . . . teaching them to
> obey everything that I have commanded you.
> —*Matthew 28:19-20*

> All scripture is inspired by God and is useful for teaching, for reproof,
> for correction, and for training in righteousness, so that everyone who
> belongs to God may be proficient, equipped for every good work.
> —*2 Timothy 3:16-17*

The Word of God creates a world in which the whole church lives. It nourishes us like food and drink. The Word gives us language, and fluency in that language allows us to hear God more clearly and to speak God's Word more effectively in our own words and works. The Word shapes our lives individually and together as the church of Christ. This is asserted in the ELCA Confession of Faith:

> This church accepts the canonical Scriptures of the Old and New Testaments as the inspired Word of God and the authoritative source and norm of its proclamation, faith, and life.[7]

The nouns *proclamation, faith*, and *life* are not meant to be separated, but point to various ways the life of this church is to be normatively shaped by the Word.

Our proclamation—Whoever undertakes to speak in God's name is to use the norm of Scripture. ELCA congregations, synods, assemblies, staff, members, agencies, and ministries will test words of demand and promise against the Bible. We expect of one another a fluency that allows God's law and gospel to be heard. Lutherans are confident that God speaks through people, today as always, but the Bible is the source and norm that allows us to speak to and hear one another with confidence.

Our beliefs—As the ELCA, the focus of our trust and our formulations of the faith are determined by Scripture. The creeds, confessions, and doctrines of the church are normative for us because and in so far as they are faithful explanations and summaries of God's Word in Scripture. We expect all attempts at fresh formulation to proclaim the same faith and to convey freely the Word's demand and promise.

Our life—The Bible shapes individual behavior, and it shapes the ELCA's institutional life. It determines our commitment to evangelizing, to gathering for worship, to teaching the faith. The Bible calls this church to have structures and policies that leave God free to speak. Institutionally and individually, we seek to take due account of sin and of God's justifying power. We have confidence that God is at work in the day-to-day reality of the church as the body of Christ. This church is an advocate in situations where it has collectively concluded that the Scripture calls for such advocacy. So, for example, social statements of the ELCA will reflect careful study of the whole witness of Scripture. We are realistic people because the Bible teaches us that sin is pervasive. We are hopeful people because the Bible shows us a God of hope. We respect all people and the world around us because the Bible shows us God who claims and loves all.

The Bible will shape our proclamation, our faith, and our lives. The Evangelical Lutheran Church in America expects this impact on itself. We hope others will see it in us. Being shaped by the Bible is part of our identity as a Lutheran church and, individually, as Lutheran Christians.

A word of caution is necessary here. The Bible shapes this church and our individual lives, but we remain dependent upon listening to the Word of God. We can never think that we have determined precisely how Christians will live and organize. Scripture is the source and norm, not our understandings of Scripture. In speaking, in formulating doctrine, and in guiding lives, Lutherans act with confidence because we are convinced God does engage and guide us in all these arenas. However, we never place our understandings of God's Word on a par with Scripture. We are not in control. God speaks through individuals and through the church and its institutions, but only the Bible is the fully reliable standard. In the spirit of debate, even Martin Luther may occasionally have forgotten to maintain humility about his own understandings, but humility about our certainties comes from our conviction that it is God who speaks.

Thus Lutherans have always understood that church traditions and beliefs, including the Creeds, the Augsburg Confession, the Small Catechism, and other Lutheran confessional documents, are only normative because and to the extent that they rightly convey the Word of God found in the Bible. Similarly, church practices and policies, moral pronouncements, particular sermons, commentaries and devotionals, liturgies, hymns, and other human productions are all subordinate, though they are wonderfully useful for God's purpose. Clearly, this subordination applies to all our interpretations of the Scripture. The Lutheran test is the one already mentioned several times: are these words heard as God's law and gospel?

Who answers that test question? It is not up to each individual alone. Martin Luther was an outspoken critic who challenged centuries of accepted churchly interpretations. We who are his descendants do not forget the world-changing impact of his solo voice, but we always assert that the Bible belongs to the whole church—the church across the centuries and around the globe. Questions about faithfulness are discussed in community—one believer with another, as a congregation, as a denomination, and in larger gatherings. Because churchly understandings, no matter how old and well accepted, never stand on a par with God speaking in Scripture, the voice of a single Christian may proclaim a unique new insight. However, no Christian voice can individually claim the right to overturn tradition. Luther was vindicated by broad acceptance of his Scriptural discoveries, not by the power of his arguments. Strong consensus deserves attention but always stands under the Word.

It might appear ironic that Lutherans have such confidence in the Word of God and also such humility about our ability to hear the word with precision. But, in fact, these two must go together. The Word of God is not something that we possess. It always belongs to God. Naming the authority of Scripture is a declaration about the Bible and about God. Language of biblical authority is pointedly not about our self-confidence to speak for God. Our confidence is humble, and it is expectant.

Expectantly Opening the Potent Book

> Let the word of Christ dwell in you richly; teach and admonish one
> another in all wisdom; and with gratitude in your hearts sing psalms,
> hymns, and spiritual songs to God. And whatever you do, in word or
> deed, do everything in the name of the Lord Jesus, giving thanks to
> God the Father through him.
> —*Colossians 3:16-17*

> Let anyone who has an ear listen to what the Spirit is saying to the
> churches.
> —*Revelation 3:22*

In opening the Bible—the book of faith that norms all of life—Lutherans are
not doubtful and wary. Rather we practice expectancy. The Spirit is at work.
We recognize the power of the Word of God and know that powerful things
must be handled with care. The goal of this care, however, is not to protect
us, our institutions, or our interpretations but to allow the power to do its
intended work. The Word of God through the Bible must have free course
to be law and gospel for the good of sinful people. We approach the biblical
texts not with fear or doubt but with the expectant readiness appropriate to
faith in God who speaks in Jesus Christ. We intend to let the word of Christ
dwell richly in us through Scripture so it can change our lives and this world.

With our Lutheran assumptions about the Word of God and about
the Bible as the instrument of that Word, we choose ways of opening the
Bible that recognize the nature of its authority. We will not use methods
that assume the Bible is an effective substitute for God. Nor will we assume
that our insights and conclusions from this opened book could stand
without the Bible as the continuing norm. In chapter 2, Mark Allan Powell
will explore Lutheran insights that open up the Bible. In chapter 3, Diane
Jacobson will guide us through methods of Bible study that are faithful to
Lutheran convictions.

In approaching Scripture, the expectancy of faith is foundational. We
are confident that God will speak through the texts we hear. Neither prior

cautions nor present frustrations about difficult and disputed hearings should distract us from that confidence.

Expectancy shows itself in Lutheran practice. Lutheran worship has a dual focus grounded in the Word. We *proclaim* the biblical Word, and we *celebrate* Baptism and Holy Communion with their empowering biblical texts. The ELCA understands proclamation of the Word in a broad sense:

> Proclamation of the Word includes the public reading of Scripture, preaching, teaching, the celebration of the sacraments, confession and absolution, music, arts, prayers, Christian witness, and service. The congregation's entire educational ministry participates in the proclamation of the Word.[8]

The language of Lutheran worship itself is intentionally and richly drawn from the Bible. Within all this breadth, Lutherans have historically given prominence to the sermon in worship and to the study of the Bible by the people of the church. The commitment to hearing Scripture is made plain from the beginning of the Christian life. Parents and others bringing children for baptism are reminded of their responsibilities that include "to live with them among God's faithful people . . . (and) place in their hands the holy scriptures . . . ."[9] Confirmands and others affirming their baptismal covenant are asked about their intent . . . "to live among God's faithful people, hear the word of God and share in the Lord's Supper. . ."[10]

The commitment to hearing the Word shapes both communal and individual Christian practices. Daily Bible reading is encouraged so that God's Word can shape our lives and guide our decisions. For Lutherans, individual use of daily lectionaries, devotional guides, and disciplines such as *lectio divina* and meditation are always understood as taking place within the context of the whole community of faith. This context reflects our conviction that God's Word is for all and is never a private possession.

Lutheran convictions lead to use of the Bible for proclamation, worship, study, and discernment so that the Word of God may speak to others and to us. The assumptions and approaches mentioned here and in the following chapters are certainly not unique to Lutherans, but they reflect our convictions about the Scriptures. We are shaped by the certainty that God speaks through the Bible. That leads us to expectant stewardship of the Bible and to humility about our claims and conclusions.

Human Obstacles to God's Powerful Word

> Beloved, do not believe every spirit, but test the spirits to see whether they are from God; for many false prophets have gone out into the world. By this you know the Spirit of God: every spirit that confesses that Jesus Christ has come in the flesh is from God, and every spirit that does not confess Jesus is not from God.
> —1 John 4:1-3a

Not all practices for approaching the Bible are helpful. Lutherans must question and even challenge some. Some approaches do not reflect our conviction that the Bible is the means of God's grace. Such objectionable approaches include any that treat the Scriptures as though the authority belongs to the words alone, rather than to the God who speaks and engages us through the text. Conversely, some other approaches are questionable because they ignore the truth that God has chosen to speak through human words and human writers.

Approaches to Scripture can intentionally or carelessly suggest that the reader or some method is in control of the meaning. This error may be revealed when an interpreter or group implies that their particular understanding must be correct and shows disrespect for the faithfulness of others' efforts at hearing. Our understandings of God's engagement must demonstrate both confidence in the God who speaks and humility about our own wisdom, knowing that the gift of the Bible is given to the whole church. Our hearing does not take priority over God's voice, but God does address us. The test, as 1 John says, is whether our approaches allow the Spirit of God to point us to Jesus Christ come in the flesh. The Word is for this human world, but it remains God's Word.

Reading the Bible without community can be problematic. Every Christian is called to hear the texts in his or her life. Small circles of Christians are to hear the texts for their own context. Difficulties arise when that hearing is disconnected from the whole community of Christ. Readings without community can cause despair. One must hear the gospel from another person; one cannot simply proclaim it to oneself. Readings without community can also be arrogant, carelessly assuming that God has revealed a truth not shown to anyone else. Of course, a unique insight may be from God, but insights are always tested by discernment within the larger Christian community, including the community that stretches back across the centuries and around the globe. Lutherans will doubt any approach that claims certainty without being in continual conversation with the whole community of the book of faith.

Reading the Bible without its contexts must be rejected. God has chosen to be self-revealed through human memories and understandings passed on and put into human writings, collected and preserved by humans. This means that we must consider the vocabulary and grammar of ancient peoples. We must pay attention to literary customs, forms, and contexts. We need to know the history of the community of faith and of the text. Ripping words from their God-chosen environment risks mishearing the voice of God. The words of the Bible do not stand on their own without the God who inhabits them. Particular sentences are not disconnected from the rest of the Bible or from the God who inspires them. The life and teachings of the church can be grounded in nothing but the grace of God.

Biblical reading without expectancy or limited expectancy may be the most dangerous misreading of all. We may not really expect God to address us, or we may place conscious or unconscious limits on what we expect to hear. Lutherans know that God speaks to all of life—to each of us in all the callings of our daily lives. Yet we often fail to expect the full breadth and power of God's Word. For example, Christians can be subject to a narrow expectancy, as though the Bible speaks only to a part of life we call "religious" or "spiritual." The Bible is for Monday as well as Sunday. Another inadequate expectancy misunderstands the integration of law or the gospel in God's speaking. On the one hand, some miss the life-challenging power of God's Word by expecting the Bible to be only a collection of rules and guidelines that can be mastered. On the other, some miss the future orientation of the gospel, seeing the gospel only as a comfortable release from past wrongs. Some seek only glorious and uplifting messages from the Bible—reading as though Christ has not been crucified and as though the Bible does not present God at work even in the midst of sin and evil.

Biblical reading without care and attention to the nature of the Bible can limit the Bible's effective authority for us. The Bible, after all, is an ancient and complex book. Even with good translations, the language and imagery are often unfamiliar to us. Consider this analogy: Imagine a person walking into a large public library or into a bookstore for the very first time. Should that person begin reading the first book on the top shelf of the first bookcase to the right and continue through the whole collection in sequence? Likely not. The person needs an orientation and probably some companions for guidance to use such book collections fruitfully. Similarly, the Bible is a collection of writings, a library. An orientation and companions can be essential. Similarly, as with the individual books in a library or bookstore, the books of the Bible will speak much more clearly if we have help. Though Lutherans confidently believe that God speaks through the Bible to each and all, we also believe that the interpretive guidance of other Christians can be a gift of God. Some of these guides may be experts. Some will be other faithful hearers, some more experienced than we. The Bible is fundamentally clear. It speaks in its plain sense, and we are wise to read it together. Because we understand that Bible is given to the whole church, we open ourselves to the wisdom of others. Collaboration is a vital aspect of allowing God to engage us through the Scriptures.

Diverse and conflicting interpretations often obscure the authoritative function of the Bible. We see disagreements about Scripture between individuals, within congregations, in denominations, and across global Christianity. Some of this diversity may come from laziness, carelessness, or ignorance, but most often the conflict arises between interpretations by believers who are equally committed to the authoritative texts and who are equally diligent at being open to God's voice in Jesus Christ. Disagreement is not new. Disagreements have been part of faith's experience since the very beginning. The Bible itself reports disputes amongst God's people about God's Word. Nevertheless, seeing such disagreements, ancient or modern, can make us uncomfortable and threaten our confidence in God's speaking. It can undermine the authority of the Bible for us. We wonder why God does not resolve our differences. In the face of divergent interpretations, Lutherans will consider carefully whether we are asking the right questions and, more importantly, whether we are respecting the nature of the Bible's authority. Are we trying to control Scripture and force it to answer our questions, or are we—more faithfully—allowing Scripture to question us? The Lutheran conviction that God speaks in Scripture as demand and promise does not support the notion of a Bible that will answer every question and problem we bring to it. We do not say to God or to the Bible, "Solve this! Resolve this!" However we may prayerfully say, "We and our sisters and brothers are in perplexity, and we seek to listen intentionally to your Word. Guide us by your Spirit."

Our anchor in facing the challenges of conflicting interpretations is the same foundational belief: God in Jesus Christ speaks through the Bible. The Spirit of God guides us in our hearing. Thus, we return to the texts. The Bible is the fixed point given to us. It is the norm. Our commitment to this authority leads us to treat any Christian disagreement as a conversation that remains open. We take that stance, remembering the fundamental Lutheran assumption that the Bible speaks clearly. Until we hear clearly, we seek to be patient. God does speak. The Word interprets us, so we stand before it in hope, with our varied understandings. "Now we see in a mirror, dimly, but then we shall see face to face" (1 Cor 13:12). We remain expectant. And we challenge those who have lost their expectancy to join us in hope. As Lutherans, we will rely on the approaches to Scripture that have proven so fruitful for generations. We commend them to others. We listen in confidence.

In a church that is confessionally committed to the Bible as its norm and rule, we are stuck with it. We may consider this situation with gnashing teeth and clenched fist as our being condemned to live with a hopelessly flawed source of authority forever. Alternatively, we can regard the need to struggle with this uncomfortable Bible as a privilege, a chance for ever new discoveries and ever new beginnings in the dialogue the living, eternal God has initiated for our benefit.[11]

Finally, of course, a continuing challenge to the authority of the Bible is neglect. God cannot speak through words that are unread, unheard, unknown. In the community of faith, such neglect is never absolute, of course. The words of God's powerful book are always there, and God finds ways to be heard. Yet sin infects even our faithful attention to the Bible's authority and our ability to intend such attention. Communally and individually, God invites us to hear, again and again. From the ancient Middle East of Ezra and Nehemiah, through the Europe of Martin Luther, to our present day in a global community, God's people are renewed when they are called back to the Word that has been neglected. We initiate such a call with expectancy. The Bible is a book of faith.

God's Invitational Book

> Ho, everyone who thirsts, come to the waters;
> And you that have no money, come, buy and eat!
> Come, buy wine and milk without money and without price.
> —Isaiah 55:1

> Philip found Nathanael and said to him, "We have found him about whom Moses in the law and also the prophets wrote, Jesus son of Joseph from Nazareth. Nathanael said to him, "Can anything good come out of Nazareth?" Philip said to him, "Come and see."
> —John 1:45-46

This chapter began with words of the prophet Isaiah, proclaiming the life-giving power of God's word. It appropriately comes to a conclusion with Isaiah's invitation, from the beginning of that same prophetic speech, inviting the inattentive crowds, "Come!" Such an invitation was issued by one of Jesus' first followers as he invited his doubtful brother, "Come and see!" The Bible is an invitational book, welcoming people to hear the voice of God. Lutherans will intentionally relay the Bible's invitation and respond themselves.

> The church today would do well to follow the example of Luther and the Confessions, whose efforts focused less on defending the status of the Bible than on using the Scriptures, through translation and evangelical interpretation and preaching, for the sake of the church and the world.[12]

The nature and workings of biblical authority do interest Lutherans.[13] Debates about Scripture can serve the primary purpose of the Bible, nurturing faith. But such debates can also distract us and derail trust. Our foundational concern is that the Word be heard.

Lutherans take initiative for the hearing of the Bible—for ourselves and for others. We intend to be a church of the Bible, to make the Scriptures available and accessible to our own members of all ages, and to share the Word as a missional church with a public voice. This *Opening the Book of Faith* volume has its roots in the Book of Faith Initiative of the Evangelical Lutheran Church in America. The vision of this initiative is, "That the whole church become more fluent in the first language of faith, the language of Scripture, in order that we might live into our calling as a people renewed, enlivened, and empowered by the Word."[14]

Opening the Book of Faith is offered as an invitation to experience the Bible as a book of faith. God invites us, individually and together, to listen expectantly to the words of the Bible, listening in the company of others who help us hear. By the Spirit's power, we will hear the Word of God.

Open Scripture. Join the conversation.

2. How Can Lutheran Insights Open Up the Bible?*
Mark Allan Powell

This chapter is going to focus on how Lutherans approach the Bible. Let me begin by saying a word to my Lutheran readers and, also, a different word to any non-Lutherans who might be reading this volume (I hope that there are many of you!).

First, although I am a Lutheran pastor and a Lutheran Bible professor, I cannot possibly speak for all Lutherans. I can't even speak for all ELCA Lutherans. At best, I can only try to describe what is *typical* and *traditional* for Lutherans. If your understanding of the Bible is different from what I offer here, that does not mean that you are a bad Christian—or even a bad Lutheran. One thing that Lutherans believe is that *not everyone needs to be typical or traditional*. We are bigger than that.

Next, for the non-Lutherans, let me point out that much of what I have to say in this chapter might be true of your church also. Lutherans are not *peculiar* in how they understand the Bible. We don't have some weird way of using Scripture that separates us from everyone else. Most of what we do is pretty similar to what other Christians do, but we sometimes do put a little different spin on things. We have our priorities and our preferences, and these sometimes lead us to understand Scripture differently.

Also, I have to say that I really *like* what Lutherans do with the Bible. I try to be respectful of all churches and, as a scholar, I try to maintain a certain degree of academic objectivity when talking about these matters—but I fear I do not do that very well. I don't want to say that Lutherans are better than everybody else in their approach to the Bible, because that would be rude. But, even if I don't *say* it, I might think it, because I am a Lutheran and I really like what we do. I like that "spin" that we put on things.

* Portions of this chapter are adapted in part from Mark Allan Powell's *How Lutherans Interpret the Bible,* © 2006 SELECT Multimedia Resources. www.elca.org/select

The Word of God

Perhaps the first and last thing I want to say about Lutherans and the Bible is this: Lutherans believe the Bible is the Word of God. Of course, almost all Christians would say this—and they might mean all sorts of different things by it. So we have to ask: What does it mean to say the Bible is the Word of God? Simply put, it means that the Bible tells us what God wants to say. Things are going to get more complicated than that, but let us begin with that obvious affirmation: We Lutherans believe that the Bible tells us what God wants to say to us.

In the last chapter, we read that our ELCA constitution says that we accept the Bible as "the inspired Word of God and the authoritative source and norm of its proclamation, faith, and life." Thus, when people ask me what Lutherans believe about the Bible, I try to use those words. I say, "We believe the Bible is the Word of God"; we believe it is the *inspired* Word of God; we believe it is the *authoritative* Word of God."

But sometimes that is not enough, and people want to ask me other things. They ask me questions that I do not always know how to answer.

Someone says, "Do you believe the Bible?" I say, Yes, I do. "*Literally?*" they ask. "Do you believe it *literally?*"

I'm not sure how to answer that. I believe the literal parts literally. And I believe the metaphorical parts metaphorically. When the Bible says, "The Lord is my Shepherd" (Ps 23:1), I believe that, but I don't think that I believe it *literally*. If the Lord were literally my Shepherd then wouldn't I have to be a literal sheep? And I'm not.

The Bible says that God is a rock (Ps 18:31). I believe that. But I don't believe it literally.

And then someone will ask, "What about errors? What about contradictions? Do you believe the Bible is *inerrant*?"

Again, I'm not sure how to answer, because I'm not always sure what *they* mean by errors. Scientific errors? Jesus said the mustard seed is the smallest of all seeds (Mark 4:31). Scientists tell me that orchid seeds are smaller. Is that a horticultural error? Or maybe Jesus was just talking to people who would never see an orchid, so the mustard plant had the smallest seeds as far as they were concerned. How far do we want to press this question of "errors"?

How about grammar? There's one place in the Sermon on the Mount where Jesus warns his disciples to beware of wolves in sheep's clothing. He says, "You will know them by their fruits" (Matt 7:16). How, exactly, do you recognize a wolf by its fruit? Wolves don't have fruit. My seventh-grade grammar teacher would have called that a "mixed metaphor." If Jesus had written it in her class, she would have marked it with red ink—called it a grammatical error and made him do it over.

But these things don't bother me—and they don't bother most Lutherans. There are churches for which these things are very important, and people write big books explaining why things that look like errors in the Bible aren't really errors and why things that look like contradictions aren't really contradictions. The point is to *defend* the Bible as accurate and reliable and true. Not many of these books are written by Lutherans because that is not usually what interests us. The difference lies in what we mean when we say "the Bible is the word of God." We do not mean, "the Bible is a book that contains no errors or contradictions." We mean, "the Bible is the book that tells us what God wants to say to us." That puts a different spin on things.

For the most part, Lutherans are more interested in *understanding* the Bible than they are in *defending* it. We don't think that we have to *prove* the Bible is the word of God—we just believe that it is the Word of God, and then we focus on asking, "What *does* God have to say to us?"

Again, I cannot speak for all Lutherans, but I will tell you what I think. I think that the Bible says exactly what God wants it to say. Every book of the Bible, every chapter of the Bible, every verse of the Bible says *exactly* what God wants it to say. So, if there are contradictions or errors or whatever you want to call them in the Bible, it's because God wants them to be there or allows them to be there. Either way, when we read the Bible, it tells us what God wants to say to us. And that is what I care about: hearing the Word of God.

But let us move on. Lutherans have more to say about the Word of God—and it is really good stuff. As Stan Olson indicated in our last chapter,

Lutherans typically speak of "the Word of God" in a *three-fold sense*. The Word of God is, first, Jesus Christ (the Incarnate Word); second, the message of law and gospel (the proclaimed Word); and, third, the Bible (the written Word). This, again, is in the ELCA constitution (see pages 5-6).

It isn't just Lutherans who speak of "the Word of God" this way. The Bible itself does so.

First, the Bible speaks of *Jesus Christ* as the Word of God. In John's Gospel, we read, "In the beginning was the Word and the Word was with God and the Word was God" (John 1:1). And, then, a little bit later, John's Gospel says, "The Word became flesh and lived among us" (John 1:14). Obviously, the Bible did not become flesh and live among us. Jesus Christ did. So Jesus Christ is the Word of God.

Second, the Bible speaks of *preaching* as the word of God. In the book of Acts, we often hear about Peter or Paul or some other missionary preaching "the word of God" (see, for example, Acts 13:5; 18:11). What did they do? They didn't just read the Bible to people. they proclaimed a message that convicted people of their sin and offered them hope of salvation. Lutherans call this "the message of law and gospel," and we will say more about it later in this chapter. Thus, the message of law and gospel may also be identified as "the word of God."

And, third, the Bible identifies the Scriptures as the word of God. For example, when Jesus believes that some people are failing to abide by one of the Ten Commandments, he tells them that they are "making void the word of God" (Mark 7:13). Jesus did not just regard Scripture as ancient testimony, as a collection of old traditions that ought to be valued for their historical significance. He believed that the writings of Scripture continued to express what God had to say to people centuries after they were written. Thus, the writings of Scripture may be identified as the word of God.

Not many people will argue with this idea of the three-fold word of God, but some might wonder why it matters. Are we simply using the same phrase for three different things? No, we would say that they are *not* three different things but three different representations of the same thing.

When the Christian missionaries preached the message of law and gospel, they revealed the same truth that Jesus Christ revealed when he became flesh and lived among us. Likewise, when we say that the Bible is the "word of God" we mean that it also reveals this same truth. The Bible functions as the word of God when it shows us Jesus Christ and conveys the message of law and gospel to us.

Sola Scriptura

Lutherans say that Scripture is the "only rule and norm" according to which doctrines are to be established and evaluated. This does not mean that Lutherans do not respect the validity of sound reason or the legitimacy of human experience. Rather, Scripture has unique authority as the only record of *revealed* truth, and it therefore provides a perspective from which human reason and experience are best understood.

The phrase *sola scriptura* became something of a rallying cry for Lutherans in the sixteenth century. It literally means "scripture only" or "scripture alone." But what does *that* mean? Obviously, Lutherans don't believe *only* things that are in the Bible. There is very little math in the Bible, but we don't have anything against mathematics. What exactly do we mean by saying "scripture alone"?

I think it helps to use the analogy of a three-legged stool. Christian philosophers have often said that a stool needs three legs to stand up. Actually, it could have four legs or five legs and still stand up, but the point is that a stool with only one leg or only two legs would fall over.

Secular or pagan philosophy often claims that there are two primary sources for knowing the truth: *reason* and *experience*. We believe some things are true because they are logical and rational. We believe other things are true because experience and observation reveal them to be true. But *Christian* philosophers sometimes claim that this is only a two-legged stool. If you take everything that it is possible to know through reason and experience, you still do not have a sturdy or reliable grasp of the truth. There is a third leg: *divine revelation*. We know certain things to be true because God has revealed them to us.

Let's consider two examples of things that most Lutherans probably believe are true. First, most of us probably believe that tadpoles, if they live long enough to mature, will turn into frogs. The Bible does not teach this, so why do we believe it? Well, people have observed thousands of tadpoles over the years and, so far, none of them have turned into turtles. They have all turned into frogs and, so, it is only logical to assume that the ones we have not yet observed will turn into frogs also. So, we believe this on the basis of reason and experience.

But most of us also believe that when we eat the bread and drink the wine of Holy Communion, we receive the body and blood of Christ. This is not particularly logical, and it is not something that can be shown to be true through scientific observation or analysis. Our experience does not always point to this truth: the wine doesn't *taste* like blood and, after receiving Holy Communion we don't necessarily *feel* like we have got more of Jesus in us than we did before. Why do we believe such a thing? By virtue of divine revelation. God has told us that we receive Christ through this meal and we believe that it is true.

Okay, so what do Lutherans mean by *sola scriptura*? They mean that scripture alone has authority to constitute that third leg, to serve as a source of divine revelation. Not councils. Not popes. Not churchwide assemblies. Not bishops or seminary professors. Only the Bible has the authority of divine revelation.

Thus, we are not rejecting experience or reason. We are not saying, "The stool should have only one leg." There are Christians in the world who would say that experience and reason do not matter, as long as you have the Bible on your side. That is often the view of fundamentalism.

But Lutherans are not fundamentalists—at least not typically or traditionally. We do not reject experience or reason, but view them as appropriate God-given avenues for knowing the truth. Still, *some* truth can only be known by revelation, and the Bible is the only source for that truth.

But now someone will ask, "What happens when the Bible contradicts reason or experience? What happens when they don't agree?" That's a difficult question, and not all Lutherans would answer it the same way. To some extent, it depends on the topic—what, exactly, are we talking about? The Bible makes claims about Jesus Christ that fly in the face of human wisdom. The Apostle Paul says that the very idea of God saving people through a cross is "foolishness" to this world (see 1 Cor 1: 18-25). Likewise, the notion that people should die to self-interest and become servants of others contradicts much conventional wisdom regarding what it means to be successful in life (see Mark 8:34-35; 10:43-45; Phil 2:4-7).

In many matters, however, if I think that what the Bible teaches contradicts sound reason or human experience, I have to wonder whether I've missed something. Basically, I feel like the stool is a bit wobbly or out of balance. God does not expect us to just turn off our brains and believe things that don't make any sense or that don't pan out in reality. If believing the Bible forces me to do that, I at least want to go back and see if I've missed something. It is at least possible that I did not understand the Bible properly.

So, Lutherans do not view the Bible as the only source for knowing what is true in this world, but they do claim that the Bible is the only authoritative source for knowing divine truth that God reveals to us.

Understanding the Bible

Lutherans *read* the Bible . . . they *believe* the Bible . . . they *love* the Bible. But they also try to *understand* the Bible. Understanding might not be as much fun as reading, believing, and loving. In fact, it can be a lot of work. Still, it *is* pretty important (see Matt 13:23), and Lutherans have earned a reputation for being Christians who emphasize *understanding*.

We are going to look at some principles that Lutherans have come up with to guide them in understanding the Bible. But, first, let's consider a basic question: "Where did we get the Bible?" Where does the Bible come from?

We can answer the question, "Where does the Bible come from?" in three ways: two simple answers and one complicated answer.

The first simple answer is "The Bible comes from God." We are not being naive by saying that. Of course, the Bible did not just fall out of heaven, all bound in leather with the words of Jesus printed in red. But it *is* the Word of God, and it does convey what God wants to say to us in a way that no other book or collection of books ever could. Lutherans have no trouble saying, "This book comes from God."

And the second simple answer is, "The Bible comes from the church." The church (meaning the historic Christian church) put the Bible together, preserved it, translated it, and made sure that people like you and I could have copies of the Bible today. The Bible is the church's gift to us and to the world. This is kind of ironic because I have noticed that not everybody who likes the Bible likes the church. In fact, people sometimes contrast the two. I hear people say, "I don't care what the church thinks—I only care about what the Bible says." But the Bible comes from the church. We know that the Christian church has had a strange and not always noble history. It has done a lot of things wrong over the years. But *this* is one thing the church did right. The church gave us the Bible.

So, those are two simple answers: the Bible comes to us from God, through the church. The more complicated answer is that the individual books of the Bible—all 66 of them—were written by human beings, flesh and blood people like us. If you want the complete answer for where all these books come from, you might have to take classes somewhere—or read 66 different chapters in some Bible study textbook—because the answer would be different for almost every book.

So what? This is important for Lutherans because we believe the Bible must be studied and interpreted if we are going to understand it and receive God's truth. There is a famous bumper sticker that reads, "God said it, I believe it, and that settles it." Lutherans would want it to be a little bit longer: we would want to say something about *understanding* what God has said. It doesn't do any good to believe what you think the Bible teaches if you have misunderstood what the Bible teaches. What would we want the bumper sticker to say? "God speaks to us through the Bible, we interpret the Bible to understand what God wants to say, and then we believe it—and *that* settles it." But, of course, that is much too long. Lutherans have never been very good at bumper stickers.

But we *are* pretty good at biblical interpretation. Of course, lots of things in the Bible are perfectly clear. "Be kind to one another" (Eph 4:32). "Do not commit adultery" (Exod 20:14). Those verses are pretty straightforward and, in these cases, the teaching of the Bible is not hard to understand. It might be hard for some people to *follow*, but it is not hard to understand.

Other things in the Bible are very difficult. You can get twenty Ph.D.'s in a room and have twenty different opinions as to what a particular text means.

So, Lutherans believe the Bible can be misunderstood. We not only believe that it *can* be misunderstood. We believe that it *has* been. The Bible was used to support slavery in this country. It has been used to oppress women. It has been used to stir up hatred against Jews and Muslims. The people who burned witches in Salem and the people who burned crosses in Selma had one thing in common: they were absolutely certain that God was on their side, and they could quote Bible passages to prove it.

But, of course, it's easy to wag our heads over those foolish, misguided people. What about *us*? Well, Lutherans have not always gotten this right either! Still, we have learned one thing over the years: anytime that you are absolutely certain that God is on your side, it may be good to get a second opinion. We need to listen to each other, and we especially need to listen to those who don't agree with us.

If *we* think that the Bible means something, and there are other people—Christian people who love and worship Jesus—who think that the Bible means something else, maybe we should talk to each other. Lutherans are *really* big on "listening" and on "talking to each other." We call it "dialog" and it is one of our favorite words. If you want to make fun of Lutherans, that's probably where to go. We're always having dialogues. And drinking coffee.

Five Key Lutheran Principles

But what I want to do now is look at five key principles Lutherans follow when they study or interpret the Bible. The principles are easier to describe than they are to practice, but we have discovered over the years that when we do manage to follow these principles, we usually get things right.

1. LAW AND GOSPEL

Lutherans say that the Word of God speaks both law and gospel and that both must be held together for God's Word to be fulfilled. One way to describe these important terms is:

- the *law* is that which accuses us and judges us;
- the *gospel* is that which comforts us and saves us.

This message of law and gospel is at the heart of Scripture: faithful interpretation discerns this message; faithful proclamation declares this message.

Lutherans talk a lot about *law* and *gospel*, and there are many books that try to define what these terms mean and what they include. But in a basic sense we are simply saying that the Bible speaks God's word to us, and that this is always a word of judgment and salvation. It is a word that condemns us and redeems us. We are poor, human sinners, so God's word always condemns us, but our God is a God of love and mercy, so God's word always redeems us. Another way of saying this is, God's Word reveals our brokenness (that is the law) and it also forgives and heals our brokenness (that is the gospel).

Lutherans talk about "law and gospel" a great deal, but the expression is often misunderstood, both by non-Lutherans and by Lutherans themselves. One common misunderstanding sometimes equates "the law" with the Old Testament and "the gospel" with the New Testament. This is not right. There is a lot of material in the New Testament that accuses and judges people (law), and there is a lot of material in the *Old* Testament that comforts, saves, and heals (gospel). The whole Bible is both law and gospel.

A similar misunderstanding often tries to categorize Bible passages as *either* law *or* gospel. Some people develop lists: law texts and gospel texts. The law is usually associated with commandments, and the gospel, with promises. Why is this wrong? Because the *same* text may function as *both* law and gospel: which *function* it has in any given situation may depend upon who is reading it and on what they need to hear.

The Bible says, "The last will be first, and the first will be last" (Matt 20:16). This may be heard as a word of comfort to those who are "last" in this life (the poor, the marginalized, the oppressed, or persecuted). But it might also be heard as an accusing word of judgment to those who are "first" in this world, especially if they are people committed to doing whatever is necessary to go on being first.

Or, let us consider a well-known Bible story. Moses leads the children of Israel out of bondage in Egypt: there is a dramatic exodus, an escape through the Red Sea, and now they are free in the wilderness of Sinai. Moses goes up on the mountain and comes down with some declarations from God. Here is one of them: "I am the Lord your God . . . you shall have no other gods before me" (Exod 20:2–3). Is this law or gospel? It is certainly a commandment, and it does speak an accusing word of judgment against those who think "freedom" means they can do whatever they want (for example, worship golden calves). But there were probably many people in the crowd that day who heard this commandment as pure gospel: They had heard about numerous gods, many of whom made terrible (and conflicting) demands on their followers. How could you keep all those different gods happy? But now, Moses said, the children of Israel would have only one God: the all-powerful Lord who had loved them enough to come to them in Egypt and deliver them from bondage. That was good news! So, the same message ("you shall have no other gods") could speak an accusing word of law to some people and a comforting word of gospel to others.

Finally, another misconception about "law and gospel" is that the law is bad and the gospel is good. We don't believe that. The gospel is often more *pleasant* than the law, but both are good and important and necessary. Sometimes, we need to hear a message that makes us feel guilty and ashamed, that brings us to despair, that makes us long for God's grace and appreciate God's grace. A psalmist says, "The law of the Lord is perfect, reviving the soul" (Ps 19:7). The law does not always *seem* pleasant when it corrects and disciplines us, but it is more to be desired than gold (Ps 19:10). And if we can say this of the law, imagine what could be said of the gospel! Actually, we don't have to imagine. We can just look and see: the gospel is glorious (1 Tim 1:11); it is powerful (Rom 1:16); and it is eternal (Rev 14:6). It is more precious than life and more valuable than the whole world (Mark 8:35-36); it brings salvation to all who have faith (Rom 1:16).

Lutherans look for both messages in the Bible: law *and* gospel. This is part of what makes us love the Bible. We don't just believe the Bible; we treasure it—promises and commandments alike.

And this also says something about how Lutherans understand the Bible. We have a certain bias regarding what is most important in scripture. That is not to say that anything is *un*important. But traditionally and typically, we have our priorities.

When a Lutheran pastor looks at a text for Sunday morning, whether it's from the Old Testament or from one of the epistles, or from one of the Gospels or other biblical books, there may be all kinds of things that this text has to say to us. We might be able to learn some interesting things about agricultural practices in ancient Israel. Or, maybe the passage tells us a story about some interesting or important person who lived a long time ago.

There's nothing wrong with learning about those things, but Lutheran pastors are trained to look at texts and ask two questions: Law? Gospel? What does this text say that brings God's word of judgment? And, what does it say that brings God's word of salvation? And all Lutherans can experience God's Word more profoundly if they listen carefully for how that Word speaks to them through this double truth of law and gospel.

2. WHAT SHOWS FORTH CHRIST

When we Lutherans say the Bible is the Word of God we mean, above all, that the Bible is the book that reveals Jesus Christ to us. And by that we mean the whole Bible—not just the Gospels or the New Testament.

The Jesus we know and love is the Messiah of Israel, so the Scriptures of Israel—the Old Testament—also reveal him to us. Sometimes, I admit, this happens in a kind of a roundabout fashion. But, eventually, everything in the Bible brings us to Jesus Christ. Everything in the Bible points us toward Christ and helps us to know Christ and to love Christ and to have a relationship with Christ, who is risen from the dead.

Martin Luther used to say the Bible is like the manger that held the Christ child. In many Christmas scenes, we see people kneeling before the manger to worship, but they are not worshiping the manger. They are worshiping the Christ child who is in the manger. So, also, we do not worship the Bible. We worship the Christ who is found in the Bible.

I like to put it this way: *Lutherans are Jesus people, and they understand the Bible to be a Jesus book.* This is my own language—a contemporary way of expressing what I think is typical and traditional for Lutheranism.

Let's take the first part of the sentence first. Lutherans are Jesus people. All Christians believe in Jesus and worship Jesus, so maybe we are no different from anyone else, but for us, it's *all* about Jesus. Theologians in other denominations sometimes say that Lutherans are "Second Article Christians," by which they mean that we emphasize the "Second Article" of the Apostles' or Nicene Creed. That is a sophisticated, academic way of saying that we are "Jesus people."

Being a Christian *means* being in a relationship with Jesus Christ, who is risen from the dead. We have creeds and confessions, but we don't think that Christianity is just a lot of doctrines that people are supposed to learn and believe. We have rituals (sacraments) like Baptism and Holy Communion, but we don't think that Christianity is just taking part in rituals. Our theology, our doctrines, our sacraments, our liturgy—all of those things are important because they help us to have a relationship with Jesus Christ.

I like to say, everything is a *means to an end*, except Jesus. Knowing Jesus and being known by him, loving Jesus and being loved by him—that is what ultimately counts.

Next time you are in a Lutheran worship service, notice what happens when we read the Gospel lesson on Sunday morning. Immediately after the lesson is read, everyone responds, "Praise to you, O Christ!" They do not say, "Praise to you, O Bible!" There is a reason for that.

I tell my students at Trinity Lutheran Seminary: I hope you love the Bible, but remember this—the Bible will never love you back. Jesus will. It is Jesus who loves you, not the Bible. You cannot have a relationship with the Bible. You can have a relationship with Jesus.

But why is this a principle for understanding the Bible? Because, for Lutherans, the Bible is only a means to an end, and that does affect how we approach and interpret Scripture. For example, this principle might offer one reason for why Lutherans do not usually get upset over things like the theory of evolution (one reason—there are others). Even apart from the question of what the Bible does or does not teach on this matter, Lutherans just do not read their Bibles to learn about *science*. They read the Bible to learn about *Jesus Christ*—and about things that are related to him.

We want to know about the God of Israel who is the Father of our Lord Jesus Christ. We want to know about the Holy Spirit whom Jesus has given to us. We want to know about prayer, through which we maintain our relationship with Jesus. We want to know about morality so that we can live the way that Jesus wants us to live.

We want to know about all these things, and we *expect* the Bible to tell us what we need to know about things like this. We expect the Bible to *reveal Christ* to us. We don't really expect the Bible to teach us about geography or science or mathematics. It's not that we say the Bible is wrong on any of those matters; we just don't look to Scripture to learn about such things. The Bible is a Jesus book, not a science book.

And Lutherans are Jesus people. We do not disparage the Bible by saying that it always plays second fiddle to Jesus Christ. Rather, we value the Bible precisely because it brings us to Christ and keeps us grounded in Christ.

3. SCRIPTURE INTERPRETS SCRIPTURE

Lutherans believe that difficult passages of Scripture are to be interpreted in light of those passages that are more readily understandable, and that all of Scripture is to be interpreted in light of the Bible's central themes and motifs. We often try to reconcile what is said in one part of Scripture with what is said in other parts of Scripture, sometimes recognizing that there is tension between texts that seem to say different things. We try to be faithful to the entire Bible rather than just picking some parts and leaving others alone.

This can be a lot of work. It is one reason why Lutheran pastors need to go to seminary: they need to know enough about "the Bible as a whole" to be able to interpret individual passages in a way that is faithful to what is taught elsewhere in Scripture. This is also why Lutherans do not like to use "proof texts"– single verses of the Bible that can be quoted to make a point or settle an argument. Sometimes "proof texts" do work—one verse says all there is to say on a subject—but lots of times (in fact, *most* of the time), there is more to the matter than can be said in one out-of-context passage. Lutherans are somewhat famous for saying, "Yes, but, the Bible *also* says . . ."

This principle of interpreting Scripture in light of Scripture keeps us from using individual verses to justify things that might not pass muster with Scripture as a whole. A Bible reader might conclude from Proverbs 13:24 that people who love their children should beat them with rods, but that would hardly be borne out elsewhere (see, for example, Matt 18:1-6; 19:13-15; Col 3:21). Or, again, individual passages of scripture might be quoted (and *were* quoted!) to justify the institution of slavery (Col 3:22-24). That institution was a social reality in the world of the Bible, and many biblical authors simply took it for granted. Still, the overwhelming witness of Scripture is one that prizes human liberation and freedom (see John 8:32; Gal 3:28; and the story of the exodus in the Old Testament). Certainly, Scripture presents "a world without slavery" as an ideal that godly people should favor.

The goal is to find the heart of Scripture so that we don't end up majoring in minors. Some religious people in Jesus' day got in trouble because they concentrated on little concerns and ignored big ones. Jesus told them, "You strain out a gnat but swallow a camel" (Matt 23:24). He claims that some things in scripture are more important than other things, and there are many verses in the Bible that indicate what some of these "more important" matters are.

- "What does the Lord require of you but to do justice, and to love kindness, and to walk humbly with your God?" (Mic 6:8)
- "In everything do to others as you would have them do to you; for this is the law and the prophets." (Matt 7:12)
- "You shall love the Lord your God with all your heart and with all your soul and with all your mind. This is the greatest and first commandment. And a second is like it: you shall love your neighbor as yourself." (Matt 22:37-39)

- "The weightier matters of the law [are]: justice, mercy, and faith." (Matt 23:23)
- "I handed on to you as of first importance what I in turn had received: that Christ died for our sins in accordance with the scriptures, and that he was buried, and that he was raised on the third day in accordance with the scriptures." (1 Cor 15:3-4)

In practice, interpreting scripture in light of scripture means that Lutherans must do some initial work at defining the teaching of "scripture as a whole" so that they will be able to interpret individual passages in light of the broader themes and overall message. When we do this, people who are not Lutheran often think that we are interpreting the Bible in light of our own theology. We understand why they think that, but *we* think that we are interpreting scripture (individual passages) in light of scripture (the Bible as a whole).

Let's look at a few examples:

How the Commandments Work. Lutherans often say that the commandments of God work or function in three ways: the *political function* of maintaining order in society, the *religious* function of showing us our need for the gospel, and the *ethical function* of teaching us right from wrong. There is no single verse of the Bible that explains this; rather, it is something that we have learned from studying all of the commandments in Scripture. Still, once we have learned this, we often find it useful for understanding individual commands. We look at such passages and ask, what does this commandment say about how society should be ordered? What does this commandment say about sin and our need for God's grace? And, what does this commandment say about our personal behavior and lifestyle?

Theology of the Cross. Lutherans believe that the death of Jesus Christ on the cross is an ultimate focal point of Scripture that reveals something profound about God's love for us and also about God's expectation for how we are to love and treat others. Jesus calls us to deny ourselves, take up *our* crosses, and follow him (Mark 8:34). The Apostle Paul calls us to have the same mind as Jesus Christ, who "humbled himself and became obedient to the point of death—even death on a cross" (Phil 2:5, 8). Lutherans try to read all of Scripture in this light. We know that there are individual passages in the Bible that promise rewards and prosperity to people (Deut 28:9-14), but we have to ask, would the person whose mind is conformed to that of the crucified Christ devote him or herself to seeking personal rewards and prosperity? No, we believe we are called to love others with unselfish devotion and to do what we can to make the world a better place—loftier goals than simply expanding our own borders (see 1 Chr 4:10) or feathering our own nest. In the same vein, a theology of the cross (taught in Scripture as a whole) tells us that God has special concern for the most vulnerable people of the earth (Isa 61:1; Luke 6:20; Jas 2:5) and that pure religion must be fundamentally oriented toward them (James 1:27).

Justification by Grace through Faith. Lutherans believe that the Bible as a whole presents God as gracious and merciful and "abounding in steadfast love" (Exod 34:6; Ps 103:8; Joel 2:13). We are unworthy sinners, but we have been reconciled with God through the death and resurrection of Jesus Christ. God sent Jesus to die for our sins, and we can be put right with God by trusting in God's grace (Rom 5:1-11; Eph 2:8). Since Scripture as a whole teaches this, we know better than to think that our own efforts or merit will improve our status with God or increase God's love for us. There are many passages of Scripture that encourage us to do good works, and we take those seriously, but we do not think that those works will enable us to earn favor with God. Interpreting Scripture in light of Scripture leads us to view the call to good works as an invitation for people redeemed by God's grace to act as the transformed, spirit-filled "new creations" that God has made them to be (2 Cor 5:17; Gal 5:22-23).

4. THE PLAIN MEANING OF THE TEXT

Lutherans say that Scripture is to be interpreted in line with its "plain sense." This means that passages are to be understood in the sense that would have seemed obvious to their original readers. They are not to be taken out of context or twisted to be read in a sense that never would have occurred to their original readers.

This comes straight from the teaching of Martin Luther and, when he talked about this, he had something specific in mind. It was popular in his day for interpreters to come up with creative ways of understanding the Bible that never would have been intended by the author. This was done by finding "secret meaning" in the Bible that no one had ever noticed before. The more creative the better!

For example, the Parable of the Good Samaritan (Luke 10:30-37) could be read as an allegory, meaning everything in the parable stood for something else. The man who fell among robbers was humanity, and the robbers were sin, death, and the devil. Humanity needs to be saved, but the priest and the Levite cannot help because they stand for good works, or sacrifices, or other things that cannot save fallen humanity. The Good Samaritan stands for Christ who does save humanity. The oil he pours over the man's wounds is the Holy Spirit. The inn is the Church and the innkeeper, the Apostle Paul. The two coins could stand for something too—and so could the donkey.

Luther hated this way of interpreting the Bible. And it wasn't because he disagreed with the point that was being made. Of course, fallen humanity is saved by Christ (not by good works or sacrifices) but that is not what *this* parable is about. That is not why Jesus told the story, and it is not why Luke put it in his Gospel. To put it another way, it is not the *plain sense* of the story that would have been obvious to those who first heard it. And, Luther would claim, if you allow this sort of thing to go on, people will find that they can make the Bible say anything they want it to say. We should stick to the plain sense of Scripture—the meaning it had for its original readers.

What about today? Do people still read the Bible in ways that ignore its "plain sense"? One example in our modern world might be the way that the book of Revelation gets treated at a certain popular level. Some books that are written about Revelation claim that modern authors are able to understand the book in a way that it never would have been understood in the first century. They do this by developing a creative system of codes and dispensations—some of them based on things they find in other books of the Bible and some based on current events or things that have happened in church history. Then, when these are applied to the book of Revelation, we get a picture of what is going to happen at the end of time.

You probably know what that picture looks like. There is going to be a great rapture when all the Christians—or at least the good Christians—get zapped up to heaven, leaving everyone else on earth to wonder where they went. And then there will be a great Tribulation, and the Antichrist will be come, and so forth . . .

If you have grown up Lutheran, you probably have not heard much about this—or, you may have only heard about it as something that people in *other* churches believe. Why? Do we think it's *wrong*? Do we think there *won't* be a rapture, or a tribulation, or an Antichrist?

That would be going too far. Lutherans have no doctrine on this—though of course, we have *opinions*, and the opinions of individual Lutherans on such matters will vary. Basically, we recognize that the book of Revelation is a difficult book to understand, and we know that intelligent, responsible people understand it in different ways. We do not endorse one way of understanding this book as right and reject other ways of understanding it as wrong.

But our tendency—what is typical and traditional for Lutherans—is to focus on how the book would have been understood by its original readers. This book was written for Christians who had suffered terrible persecution. Why had they suffered persecution? And how would this book have comforted them and helped them in their trials? Those are the questions we want to ask.

If you spend time in Lutheran circles, when you hear a sermon or Bible study on the book of Revelation, you will probably not hear about how certain things in that book match up with things that are happening in the world today, nor will you hear about what things are going to happen next, or *when* those things will happen. More likely, you will hear about how the hope of Christ's coming strengthens us and allows us to persevere and to remain faithful to God in a troubled world. The reason is that this is what we get out of the book when we pay attention to its *plain sense*—what it would have meant to its original readers.

Another possible example of "plain sense" in our modern world might be decisions as to whether images or stories are intended to be read figuratively or literally.

There are some people in our modern world who claim that stories involving supernatural occurrences ought to be read metaphorically rather than literally. For example, they will take the story of Jesus stilling the storm at sea (Matt 8:24-27) and say, "Jesus did not *really* make the storm stop; the story simply shows us how faith in Christ can help us to overcome (metaphorical) storms in our lives." Or, they will claim that Jesus did not literally open the eyes of blind people—but he opens our spiritual eyes and cures us of spiritual blindness.

The traditional Lutheran approach to interpretations like this would be to ask, how were the original readers expected to understand these stories? Again, I cannot speak for all Lutherans, but I personally think that these original readers were probably expected to take the miracle stories literally—as reports of actual events that took place in observable ways. So, I think that we should take them literally as well. Not all Lutherans would agree with me on this, but the usual Lutheran approach is to accept the "plain sense" of Scripture, or the meaning that a text would have held for its original readers.

The use of this principle presumes that we know something about the different types of material that are found in the Bible and about how those different types of material are to be understood. How did people in the first-century understand apocalyptic literature such as the book of Revelation? What did they expect to get out of a book like Revelation? How did they understand miracle stories? Figuratively or literally?

A few years ago, I was teaching a Sunday school class on the Parable of the Good Samaritan, mentioned above. I said something like, "Jesus composed this story to help people understand what it means to love their neighbor." A hand went up and a man asked, "What do you mean, he 'composed the story'? Are you saying he just made it up?"

"Well," I replied. "Yes. It's a parable."

"So, you're saying he was *lying.*"

"No, he wasn't lying—he told a parable to illustrate a point."

"But you don't think this really happened—even though the Bible says it did."

Now, I realized we had a problem. He said, "The Bible says that this man was going down the road to Jericho and fell among robbers, and then three people came along . . . but you're saying that none of that ever happened, that Jesus just made it all up and said it happened when it didn't. That makes Jesus a liar, and it means the Bible isn't true."

Well, I have to admit that's the only time I've encountered that particular concern. Most people in the church seem to think that the story of the Good Samaritan is a parable and that it really does not matter whether the events of a *parable* actually took place in history.

But I can't be too hard on this fellow. When I went to Texas Lutheran University many years ago, I had a Bible professor who told us that the story of Jonah and the big fish was a Hebrew folktale. This means, it didn't really happen. There never was a big fish—and there may not have even been a Jonah. It is just a fictional story that got put in the Bible—sort of like a parable—because people liked the point that it got across.

When I heard this, I was certain that my professor *didn't believe the Bible.* I thought he was a heretic, and I might have told him so. Now I realize that what he was saying had nothing at all to do with *believing* the Bible; it had to do with how one *understands* the Bible. That's not to say the professor was right—I still don't know about that—but if he was wrong, it wasn't because he didn't believe the Bible.

I don't personally know very much about Hebrew folktales. I do know (now) that many scholars who are experts in Hebrew literature say that, yes, the book of Jonah—the entire book—is fiction. It's a folktale, like Rip Van Winkle or the Legend of Sleepy Hollow. No one was ever *expected* to read it as an historical account, and people from that era would be amazed to learn that anybody reads it that way today. Indeed, most Jewish people have always thought this about the book of Jonah and, so, even though it appears in the prophets section of the Bible, it might seem more at home in where the book of Daniel is found. They read Jonah not as a biographical account of an historical prophet, but as a humorous folktale about a fictional prophet.

Why would they think that? In English literature, there are often clues that let us know what kind of story a particular writing is. In our day, if a story begins with the words "Once upon a time . . ." and ends with the words, "They lived happily ever after," there is a pretty good chance that the story is a fairy tale, not a news report. Jewish scholars and Christian Old Testament scholars tell me that the book of Jonah is sort of like that. It has certain characteristics that mark it as a folktale.

For Lutherans, the traditional question would be, how were people expected to understand this story in the first place? I want to make a point of this because Lutherans are often misunderstood in this regard. It comes up with other stories also, like Noah and the Ark, or Adam and Eve. Many Jewish scholars throughout the centuries have understood these stories to be folktales or fables—inspired by God, but as fictional tales rather than as historical accounts. Some Christians—including quite a few Lutherans—understand them that way also. In so doing, they are trying to read the stories the way their original readers would have read them, to uncover the meaning that the stories would have had to those readers.

5. PUBLIC INTERPRETATION

Lutherans say that the interpretation of Scripture is a public act rather than a private one. Through the Bible, God speaks to Israel and to the church. God does not speak directly or privately to individuals. What God says to Israel and to the church may have specific application for individual lives, but the meaning of Scripture for individuals is to be in harmony with its universal meaning for the community of faith.

I find that this principle is difficult for some people to grasp. We *do* encourage personal and private Bible reading, and we do believe that the Bible speaks to people as a living Word with relevance to their individual lives. But Lutherans do not believe that this just happens automatically in a magical sort of way. People do not just open their Bibles to find private messages from God, words that would apply to them in a way that they would probably never apply to anyone else.

I can relate an anecdote that might help to clarify what we mean by "private messages." I know a woman who tells me that God *does* give her private messages when she reads the Bible. She tells me that every day she opens her Bible in the morning and reads a verse and God tells her what she is supposed to do that day.

One time, she opened the Bible (King James Version) to the book of Isaiah, where it says, "He that hath no money, come buy and eat, yea come buy wine and milk without money and without price" (Isaiah 55:1 KJV). She wasn't sure what that meant, but it does mention food and wine and milk, so she decided that maybe God wanted her to go grocery shopping. She went to the grocery store and when she got there she met a friend who didn't have any money, so she bought groceries for her friend. "See," she told me, "God wanted me to go to the store that morning to help my friend, and God told me to do it through the Bible."

Lutherans would commend this woman's generosity, but they would question her interpretation of Scripture. When the prophet Isaiah spoke those words to ancient Israel, he was not telling anyone to go grocery shopping. We (Lutherans) want to know, what did the prophet Isaiah mean to say to Israel? And how does that ancient (timeless) message apply to us?

Still, when I have told this story before (with the woman's permission), I have found that some people (including Lutherans) want to support her. They will say, "How do you know God *didn't* speak to this woman and tell her to go the grocery store?" Well, of course, I don't know that. God can do anything—and God does work in mysterious ways. What Lutherans would say, however, is that we should not *count* on God doing this. We should not *expect* God to give us secret, private messages when we read the Bible.

There is an old preacher joke about a man who opened the Bible every morning to let God speak to him, and one day it said, "Judas went out and hanged himself." Hmm, he thought. I don't know what God is saying to me. So he closed the Bible and opened it again. This time it said, "Go thou and do likewise."

I actually know someone—this is *not* a joke—who was a college student and read Isaiah 55:12 for his morning devotions. It says, "You shall go out with joy." So he decided to ask a girl named Joy for a date. He was serious. He thought God had given him a private message through the Bible.

The point, I think, is that Lutherans do not treat the Bible like some kind of magic book. We don't use the Bible the way that some people use Ouija boards or horoscopes or Tarot cards.

But this does *not* mean that we think the Bible has no personal application to individual lives. Of course, it does. What we recommend is that individuals first seek the *general* meaning—what the text would mean to all people—and then ask about personal application to their own particular circumstances. What the Bible means for you should be consistent or compatible with what it means for everyone.

Some final words

We have identified some things that Lutherans typically say about the nature and authority of Scripture, and we have discussed Lutheran principles for understanding Scripture. We noted, first, that Lutherans speak of the word of God in a three-fold sense: the Bible is the written word of God, and it testifies to the same truth that was revealed in Jesus Christ (the incarnate Word) and in the message of law and gospel (the proclaimed word). Further, Lutherans say that Scripture alone has the authority of divine revelation, conveying truth that cannot be known through reason or experience.

Understanding the Bible is very important to Lutherans. In this chapter, we have described five principles that Lutherans often use to understand scripture:

We say that the Bible conveys God's message of law and gospel to us and that both law and gospel must be held together for God's Word to be fulfilled.

We try to understand Scripture in terms of "what shows forth Christ"—we are Jesus people and we read the Bible as a Jesus book.

We interpret Scripture in light of Scripture, understanding individual passages from a perspective shaped by what is taught in the Bible as a whole.

We say that Scripture is to be interpreted in line with its plain sense, in the way that it would have been understood by its original readers.

And we say that the meaning of Scripture is found through a combination of public interpretation and personal application; the Bible is God's Word to all and it should not be treated as a source for receiving private or secret messages.

These things are typical and traditional for Lutherans.

Now, I want to return to something I said at the start and attach a footnote. I said that I really like the way that Lutherans approach the Bible. That is true, but there is one thing that I *don't* like . . .

What I don't like is that many Lutherans do not approach the Bible nearly enough. Some Lutherans—probably none of you good people reading this book—but *some* Lutherans have been known to just send their children to Confirmation class and to come to church on Sunday morning and let their pastor tell them what the Bible says instead of actually reading it for themselves.

This is very un-Lutheran. Martin Luther translated the entire Bible, Old and New Testaments, into the language of the common people so that every family in Germany would be able to read the Scriptures in their homes. He was one of the first people to do this. It was a lot of work, and he did it because *he wanted Lutherans to read their Bibles in their homes.*

Lutherans today do not always take advantage of what the Scriptures have to offer. In fact, you sometimes hear Lutherans almost bragging about how they aren't "Bible-bangers" like folks in some other churches. But, truth be told, it wouldn't hurt us to bang our Bibles a bit more than we do.

We should read the Bible, we should study the Bible, we should believe the Bible, we should treasure the Bible . . . and, I think, we should even memorize Bible passages, chapter and verse.

Why? Because the Bible is the Word of God. The Bible tells us what God wants to say to us.

More than that, the Bible *does* things to us. In Scripture itself, we often hear about the Word of God as an active, dynamic force: the Word of God cleanses; it heals; it creates; it judges; it saves. One thing it does *not* do is sit unopened on bed stands or coffee tables. Rather, the Word of God is a force that never returns void but accomplishes what God intends (Isa 55:11).

So, the Bible is actually *more* than a book that says what God wants to say; it is also a book that *does* what God wants to do: a book that affects us, that transforms us.

Best of all, the Bible reveals Christ to us. It draws us into a living relationship with Jesus Christ, who is risen from the dead. Through the Bible, we come to know Jesus and love Jesus and to experience his love for us.

The Bible opens the very heart of God to us. It shows us what God has done for us—what God still does for us—what God always will do for us.

That's the first and the last thing I want to say about Lutherans and the Bible: the Bible is the Word of God.

3. How Can the Bible Be Studied?

Diane Jacobson

Introduction

As the first two chapters have expressed, we Lutherans come to our
encounter with the Bible with certain convictions and expectations. We
come not only to hear about God but also to experience God directly. We
come not only to learn about Jesus but also to meet Jesus. We come convinced, convicted if you will, that this encounter will bear fruit in our lives
for the sake of God's world. We come trusting that immersion in the Bible,
becoming more fluent in the language of the Bible, will help us live more
deeply into our calling as a people renewed, enlivened, and empowered by
the Word.

As both Stan Olson and Mark Powell have shown us, the Lutheran
understanding and experience of how this encounter works has given rise
to certain principles of interpretation that best serve our reading. The
Bible speaks to us as both law and gospel. The Bible points us to Christ
as the incarnate, crucified, and risen Lord. We start our reading with the
plain sense of a text, and we read each text in the context of the whole of
Scripture. And our interpretations are public rather than private, able to
be heard and interpreted and lived out in open conversation with the whole
church.

So, given these convictions and these principles, how might we open
the Bible ourselves and begin to read and study? Are some methods of study
more fruitful than others? Are there particular questions we can ask and
observations we can pursue that serve our convictions and open us up to
God speaking to us through the Bible?

Four Ways to Approach the Bible

In this chapter we will look at four different approaches to, or methods of, biblical study that have helped folks both today and in past generations. These are certainly not the only ways to approach the Bible, but each provides a uniquely helpful guide. The approaches can be pursued separately, or multiple questions from different methods can be and most often are used together. Each of the approaches has particular strengths that will be noted. And the approaches are not on the same order. The first three approaches are methods of reading and studying the Bible that Lutherans share with other people of faith. We share with others the conviction and hope that these ways of reading and studying can help us to hear what God is saying to us. The fourth approach gathers up the particular Lutheran insights about how the Bible works and articulates these insights as questions we might bring to our biblical study. While we share these questions about the Bible and its message with other Christians, we Lutherans have a particular stake in ensuring that such questions stand at the heart of our biblical study. The four methods we will explore are:

- Devotional Reading
- Historical[1] Reading
- Literary[2] Reading
- Lutheran Theological Reading

Together, these methodologies can be combined in one overall, inclusive approach that is represented by the chart on page 65.[3]

Notice in the diagram that the Bible is at the center. All the methods we will discuss, as well as the unified approach that combines all four methods, assume that the center point of our study and conversation is the text of the Bible itself.

Devotional Reading

Let's begin with a method that focuses on reading the text devotionally or as a meditation. This approach can be pursued either individually or in groups. The practice of meditative or devotional reading has a long history in the church and has taken many different forms.

Perhaps the oldest of these approaches is the *Lectio Divina* (Latin for "sacred reading"), a very ancient method, nurtured by the Benedictines, which can be traced far back to the patristic period (CE 100-450). This approach was intended for individual devotions, but it has been also expanded for use with groups.[4] *Lectio Divina* traditionally has four steps that can be used and adapted for many sorts of devotional reading:

- Step 1 *Lectio* (reading or listening to the text)
- Step 2 *Meditatio* (meditating, reflecting, and ruminating on the text)
- Step 3 *Oratio* (responding with prayer)
- Step 4 *Contemplatio* (contemplating and sitting quietly in the presence of God)

Let's look at each step more carefully. In Step 1 (*Lectio*) we read or listen to a biblical text. The expectation is that the text will be read aloud, carefully and deliberately. Perhaps the text can be read twice by different people who wish to read. The reading should be followed by silence, allowing each word and the passage as a whole to sink in.

In Step 2 (*Meditatio)* we meditate, reflect, and ruminate on the text. When we ruminate on Scripture we literally "chew on it" and try to "digest" its meaning. After the silence, each person might share how a word or phrase has touched his or her heart. Dysinger suggests that "Christians have always seen a scriptural invitation to *lectio divina* in the example of the Virgin Mary 'pondering in her heart' what she saw and heard of Christ" (Luke 2:19).[5] One might use any number of questions for reflection. In the past decades different groups have come up with various systems of questions that have been helpful.

One example comes from one of our Lutheran outdoor ministries. Mount Carmel Ministries suggests a T.R.I.P. method of approaching a text in its devotional publication,[6] which is based on the Moravian daily texts:

T = THANKS *What in the verse makes me thankful?*

R = REGRET *What in the verse causes me regret?*

I = INTERCESSION *What does the text lead me to pray for?*

P = PLAN OF ACTION *What action does the text encourage me to take today?*

In the seventh part of his video series called *How Lutherans Interpret the Bible,*[7] Mark Allan Powell commends two sets of questions, one from Donald S. Whitney at *The Center for Biblical Spirituality* and the second approach called SPECK, developed by David Mann. Mann suggests asking whether the passage reveals a **S**in to confess, a **P**romise to believe, an **E**xample to follow, a **C**ommand to obey, or **K**nowledge to Gain.

Two older books written for women's Bible studies suggest fifteen different ways to study the Bible with a number of helpful questions and suggestions:[8]

- What does this passage say to our world, our nation, our community, our church, to me?
- What images come to mind?
- What feelings did I have?
- What would I be concerned about if I took these words seriously?
- What person or situation would I see differently than I do now?
- What new possibility is God offering me?

These books also commend adopting the *Swedish Marking Method,* which suggests marking the text with:

- a candle for a new idea
- a double candle for a verse to memorize

- an arrow for a verse that relates to personal experience, and
- a question mark when something is not clear

Many other questions can also serve as a meditative guide:

- What scares, confuses, or challenges me in this text?
- What delights me in this text?
- What stories or memories does this text stir in me?
- What is God up to in this text?

No matter what question or set of questions might be used, having a plan, using the questions consistently over time, allowing sufficient time for contemplation, and hearing from all participants are all crucial ingredients.

In Step 3 of *Lectio Divina* (*Oratio*), we focus on responding with prayer. This step is oddly difficult for many folks. Perhaps we are out of the practice of speaking directly and personally to God from the heart. Perhaps we are used to letting pastors pray for us. In letting prayer grow out of our encounter with the text, we have an opportunity both to pray in response to our own encounter and to offer prayers for another person in the group. Beginning with prayer is the more usual practice for Lutheran Bible study. We pray that the Spirit might be present with us and through us to one another in our study of God's word.

Finally, in Step 4 (*Contemplatio*) we contemplate all we have read and heard while sitting quietly in the presence of God. Once again Dysinger is helpful:

In ancient times contemplation was not regarded as a goal to be achieved through some method of prayer, but was simply accepted with gratitude as God's recurring gift. At intervals the Lord invites us to cease from speaking so that we can simply rest in his embrace. This is the pole of our inner spiritual rhythm called contemplation. . . . We must be willing to sacrifice our "goal-oriented" approach if we are to practice *lectio divina*, because *lectio divina* has no other goal than spending time with God through the medium of His word."[9]

Lectio divina is certainly not the only possible meditative or devotional approach to Bible study, but it provides a model of structured devotions. Interestingly, Luther commends just such an approach as a spiritual practice for the formation of young theologians.[10] Luther bases his approach on Psalm 119, reduces the number of steps to three, and sets them in his own theological context that warns us against making too much of our own thinking. Luther urges us to begin with *oratio* (prayer), telling his students to "kneel down in your little room (Matt 6:6) and pray to God with real humility and earnestness, that he through his dear Son may give you his Holy Spirit, who will enlighten you, lead you, and give you understanding."[11]

"Secondly," Luther says, "you should meditate, that is, not only in your heart, but also externally, by actually repeating and comparing oral speech and literal words of the book, reading and rereading them with diligent attention and reflection, so that you may see what the Holy Spirit means by them."[12] For Luther, *meditatio* includes study, so this "devotional" approach is not separated from sound reason.

Thirdly, for Luther, there is *tentatio*, in German, *Anfechtung*. Both words are very difficult to translate, but are close to "temptation," "tribulations," or "afflictions." *Tentatio* is connected to Luther's theology of the cross. Luther here encourages us to understand that through internal and external trials we are driven to the Bible and the comfort it alone can give. He says: "This is the touchstone which teaches you not only to know and understand, but also to experience how right, how true, how sweet, how lovely, how mighty, how comforting God's Word is, wisdom beyond all wisdom."[13]

So our first approach to the study of the Bible is devotional or meditative. This practice has a pattern, happens over time, and comes with an expectation of hearing God and being engaged and transformed. The approach is rooted in prayer and coming to study with a proper attitude of openness and humility. The strength of the approach is found in the capacity of everyone to open the Scripture together and join the conversation.

You do not have or need an expert in the room. Each person is encouraged to listen well, to engage personally, and to share openly.

The next two methods arise more directly from scholarly circles and are both concerned with hearing the text in context, either historical or literary. Often these two approaches overlap. Though many believers and non-believers have used both methods to better understand the Bible, because both methods are concerned with context, they can be tied to the Lutheran interpretative principle of beginning with the plain meaning of the text. Both methods invite us to move from how the text worked through and on its original audience to how it works through and on us.

Historical Reading

A historical approach begins with the recognition that the Bible is an ancient text written by people who lived in times and places different from our own. The basic assumption of this method is that we cannot understand the plain meaning of the text without understanding something about those people, places, and times. We want to know whatever we can discover about the original situation of the text and the intentions of the author. We want to understand the historical and social world of the text. Then we work by analogy to understand how the text addresses us in our time.

An example: In speaking about the historical world, if we know something about the northern kingdom of Israel in "the days of King Uzziah of Judah and in the days of King Jeroboam . . . of Israel" (Amos 1:1), we can better understand what Amos is saying and why he said it. We can then think about similar situations in our own country and in our own time and consider if God might be issuing to us the same prophetic call for justice.

A slightly more complicated example: When reading the Gospel of Luke, we would want to know more about two historical situations. First, what was the situation in "the fifteenth year of the reign of Emperor Tiberius when Pontius Pilate was governor of Judea and Herod was ruler of Galilee" (Luke 3:1), during the time that the reported activity of the chapter happened? Second, what was happening in the last part of the first century when most Luke scholars think the Book of Luke was written? Both types of history might help us to understand Luke's presentation of John the Baptist found in chapter three. Or as a third example, in speaking about the social world of the biblical texts we are helped in understanding the importance of Paul's description in Philippians 2:7 of Christ "taking the form of a slave" if we know something about slavery as practiced in the Roman Empire. This in turn helps us to hear Paul's proclamation for our own time.

A historical approach to biblical study invites us to concentrate on who, what, why, and where questions. The underlying question would always be this: What insights from history would be helpful to know in order to hear, read, study, or understand the plain meaning of this passage more accurately?

Here are some examples of historical questions that might be asked:

- What do we know about the author, about who wrote the passage?
- Do we know to or for whom this passage was written?
- Why was this text written or what situation is being addressed?
- When was this text written and what do we know about that period of history?
- Where was this text was written and what do we know about that ancient part of the world?
- What implied political and social realities could shed light on this text?
- How is this text similar to other ancient stories or texts that might shed light on its meaning?
- What things do we know about the ancient world that might help us to read and understand this text?

The examples one could give of such historical questions and potential insights are unending. They are also often overwhelming and confusing, and this points both to the strength and the weakness of this method of study. The reality is that most people don't study the Bible with a room filled with experts or with even one expert in the room. So how can the ordinary community studying the Bible find help with this method? Here are some suggestions:

1. Be very clear about what questions you have, and then recognize that not all of these questions have answers. Certainly, not all of these questions have answers we can know. You might even consider how anyone might have answers to your questions and give up on those that you know we cannot know!

2. Know that folks with training (pastors, teachers, professors, and other trained leaders) can often be helpful. But, heavens, even scholars are not always right! Scholars often learn new things that cause us to change our minds about things we thought we knew. Scholars often deal in best theories rather than known facts. And scholars are often known to disagree. Sometimes, the more we discover, the less we are certain about what we know. Usually, our own biases have some effect on how we think and what we think we know. And, and, and . . . all of this seems quite confusing, but in truth, such confusion often deepens the meanings of texts in ways that are beyond our imagining. And this leads us to dig deeper and to try daily to hear the text more clearly. So ask folks with training to join the conversation.

3. Find and use good resources. You might begin with a good study Bible.[14] Consult accessible books from reputable publishers and written by reputable scholars. Here folks might again disagree about who is and is not reputable. Ask your pastoral leaders for reliable resources and authors. Some books may be available from your church library. Begin a structured Bible study with material designed to help with these questions.[15]

4. Keep digging. Exploring historical questions can be fun, educational, engaging, and more often than not they lead to a deeper and richer reading of the biblical text.

Literary Reading

In terms of exploring the richness and depth of the Bible, this method is equally as valuable as the Historical approach. The central aim of the Literary approach is to hear or to read a biblical text with particular attention to how the text is written, how the text conveys meaning, and how the text was and is heard. Luther and other reformers were deeply immersed in understanding the biblical text in this way, caring about the original Hebrew and Greek and reading the text with great care, attending to both the details and the logic of the argument. While the previous method was concerned with historical context, this method is concerned with literary context. Some aspects of this method overlap with the historical method and might be helped by scholarly and historical input. Primarily, this method calls on all of us to learn some helpful literary questions to put to a text and then to become careful and attentive readers who believe the details of the text matter. With each text we begin with some first steps and then move in different directions depending on the text we are studying.

Step 1. Choose a text itself with some care. Usually, one verse is too short and an entire book is too long. Choose a text with a logical beginning and ending —for example, a parable, a psalm, a set of instructions, a scene, or a whole story.

Step 2. Identify what type of literature the chosen text is. Is it a parable or psalm? Is it prophetic literature or part of a letter? Sometimes the answers are very straightforward, but this step can be more controversial than it seems at first glance. Is Jonah a prophetic book or a story? (See Mark Powell's discussion of this question in chapter 2, p. 40.) What is a Gospel? How do we describe the first chapter of Genesis? Often we get snagged by historical questions like, "Did this really happen?" Then we call the passage "history" rather than "story," and we want to read it in a different way. But the Bible is a book, or, as some have said, the Bible is really a library of sixty-six books. And even historical events are narrated, and thus can be read as one reads any narration. In this method hearing the details of *how* history is told is as important as hearing the facts.

Step 3. Read different versions of the biblical text to help discover the importance of the choices that translators make. Take care to notice how different versions express details in different ways. How do the translations alter or bring a different perspective to a word or phrase? Discovering what is said in the original Hebrew of the Old Testament or Greek of the New Testament can be important, and sometimes study notes or using a biblical concordance can help with this.[16] With this method, using more literal translations like the New Revised Standard or The New International Version is most helpful.

Step 4. Know the general themes and purpose of the book in which your passage is found. Not everyone can do this step, particularly at the outset of studying the Bible. But a group can consider together what they know about a particular book. And consulting the introduction of a book in a study Bible can be helpful.

These first steps are good starting points for studying any type of biblical literature. But subsequent questions would be different depending on whether one is reading letters or poetry or prophecy or law, etc. We will look here at questions one might ask if reading biblical narrative (such as Genesis, Exodus, Ruth, Joshua, Matthew, Mark, Luke, or John).

QUESTIONS FOR READING LITERARY CONTEXT

When you are reading a biblical narrative you might ask a whole series of questions. These are really questions you might ask when reading any novel or short story or autobiography. You do not need to be an expert, just a thoughtful and careful reader. The following are a series of sample questions about larger context, character, setting, theme, and point of view.

About Literary Context

What is the overall plot of this story, and how does this text fit into that plot?

Does the story have a structure that is like other stories, for example, a man meeting a woman at a well or a person being called by God? If so, then we can compare these stories and consider what is most important in the text in front of us.

Are there details in this text that remind us of details elsewhere in this book or other books? For example, does this text make special reference to water or clothing or food? If so, we might think about how water or clothing or food play a part throughout the Bible.

About Character

Who are the major and minor characters in this text? The major characters tend to have names, to speak, to act, and their character develops.

What do we know about each individual character? Do we learn something from the narrator or from another character, or do we intuit something about them from some detail in the text? Sometimes it is interesting to tell the story from each character's point of view and find out whom we most identify with and who draws out our sympathy, our scorn, or our admiration.

About Setting

What are the important settings in this text? Settings can be spacial, temporal, or social. Spacially, a setting might be inside, outside, or at a doorway. It might be in a temple, a palace, a tent or a city, a desert, or a river. Temporally, a setting might be a certain time of day or harvest time or deep winter or the time of a particular festival. Socially, a setting might be a banquet or a city gate or a well. Each of these settings invites us into a different world historically, symbolically, or in our imaginations.

About Theme

The details of the biblical texts in turn invite us to consider the literary themes.

What themes are highlighted in the text before us?

For example, does this text deal with violence, power, election, or morality? What is being commended and what warnings are being given? How do we know?

About Point of View

We might look at our text from a variety of viewpoints. We have spoken of the point of view of different characters.

What is the narrator's point of view? How do we know?

And climactically, what is God's point of view in this text, and how do we know?

Asking these literary questions can deepen our reading enormously. The answers will not be uniform, nor will they reveal to us a single meaning of the text, but when we begin to notice the details of how a story is told, the text can come alive in new and creative ways. Having looked at the questions we might ask about narrative, we can imagine similar questions we might ask about letters or lists of laws or other types of writing.

RELATED RHETORICAL QUESTIONS

Before we leave this method, mention should be made of a related set of rhetorical questions that invite us into an expanded perspective on the Bible. The literary questions we have asked so far center on questions that are text-based, that is, the questions all concentrate on details within the text itself. A rhetorical set of questions starts with the observation and conviction that all biblical texts are in some measure persuasive in character. That is, a text is not just analyzed or observed, it does something to the person who reads or hears it. Classical Greco-Roman rhetoric would have us observe that every situation of discourse involves the presence of three elements: the speaker (or author), the discourse (or text), and the audience (or the addressees).

Rhetorical analysis would ask how this text persuades. We might ask such questions as: Who is the speaker or author? Who is the audience or reader? How does this text work on us? At one level these questions tie us back to the historical method because we might try to answer these questions historically. But at another level, these rhetorical questions tie us to our final method of biblical study. Because we are now the audience of the text, we are the addressees. At the heart of the Lutheran notion of reading the text as law and gospel is how the Bible addresses us directly as we read the text today.

Lutheran Theological Reading

As was said at the beginning of the chapter, the first three methods are approaches to studying the Bible that Lutherans share with other Christians. But as has been made clear in the first chapters of this book, we also come to our study with certain convictions, insights, and expectations that rise particularly from our Lutheran heritage. As we encounter and are encountered by the Bible, we expect not only to learn about who God is and who Christ is, we expect to hear God and Christ speak to us directly.

LAW AND GOSPEL

Specifically, we claim that when we read the Bible, it will speak to us both as law and as gospel. This does not mean that some texts we read are always labeled law texts and some are always gospel texts but rather that when we hear or read or study the Bible, something happens to us. Asking law/gospel questions is asking about the effect of the texts on us rather than specifically about the content. We are confronted by God's law, that is, by God's demands on us, God's expectations of us, or God's judgments on us. And because we can never live up to these right and good expectations, we are driven to look to God to speak to our inadequacies, our sin, and our despair. It is then that we can be opened to hear God's gospel, God's good news of forgiveness, of grace, and of promise. So when we read any biblical text, we should ask:

- In what ways do we hear this text as law? Or how does this text speak the law to us when we hear or read or study it? What demands are being made on us? What judgments? How does this text lead us to know our own sin?
- And then, in what ways do we hear this text as gospel? How does this text proclaim the gospel to us when we hear or read or study it? How do we hear God's good news of forgiveness of our sin, of grace towards us, of promise to be with us, of the gift of Christ Jesus given for us?

These questions do not have right or wrong answers. When we ask these questions, different people will hear the text differently. And we ourselves might one day hear more law and another more gospel from the very same text. Often we will hear both. This experience of hearing law and gospel stands at the heart of what makes the Bible true for us because this experience brings us into relationship with God and with Christ.

WHAT SHOWS FORTH CHRIST

And in the midst of hearing the text as law and gospel, the text points us, drives us, leads us to Christ. Kathryn Kleinhans notes, quoting Luther, that we should expect when we read Scripture "to receive Jesus Christ 'as a gift, as a present that God has given you and that is your own'; for reading or hearing the Scriptures rightly 'is nothing else than Christ coming to us, or we being brought to him.'"[17] This conviction about the Bible is best captured by Luther's metaphor that the Bible is "the swaddling cloths and the manger in which Christ lies."[18] So when we read a biblical text, we should ask:

- In what ways does this text point us or lead us to Christ? Or how does this text prepare us for Christ? How is this text like straw in the manger where Christ lies?

Answering such questions is not always easy or evident. Understanding the gospel of Christ as the core of God's truth gives us a principle on which we can rightly take our stand, so long as we understand the cradle of Christ to contain all sorts of straw. We must be wary of applying this principle too narrowly. This Luther rarely did. Both the Old and New Testaments provide both the structure of this biblical cradle and its straw. That is, both Old and New Testament are able to show forth Christ. Demands for justice and condemnation of sin can and do show forth Christ. The psalms of faithful Israel show forth Christ. The well-placed skepticism of Ecclesiastes shows forth Christ. The good news of God's compassion, love, forgiveness, and mercy in both Testaments shows forth Christ. And difficult passages are often necessary, if uncomfortable, bedding. This question of what shows forth Christ might, like the questions of law and gospel, elicit from us stories of how the text works on us. And we might notice that the Lutheran reading and the devotional reading begin to overlap.

The final three Lutheran insights lead very directly to advice about how to read and study the Bible: letting Scripture interpret Scripture, rooting interpretation in the plain meaning of the text, and letting interpretation rise out of meanings which are public rather than private.

SCRIPTURE INTERPRETS SCRIPTURE

As Lutherans, we do not read biblical passages in isolation from each other. The whole of Scripture helps us to understand the particular and keeps passages in proper perspective. This means, of course, that the more we hear and study and know the Bible, the better able we are to find both depth and clarity of meaning. It also means that while we let each passage speak in its own voice, we judge the edges by the center. Not all passages of the Bible are equally important. Lutherans come to all Scripture with certain biblical ideas having pride of place, including justification by grace through faith and a theology of the cross. So we come to each passage with important questions that reflect these convictions:

- Can other passages in the Bible help us to understand or interpret this passage?
- Are there important ideas we find to be at the center of the Bible that help us put this passage in the perspective of the whole?

- Might we see this passage as more or less important because of our convictions about what God has done in the life, death, and resurrection of Christ?

THE PLAIN MEANING OF THE TEXT

Luther said "The Christian reader should make it his first task to seek out the literal sense, as they call it. For it alone . . . holds its ground in trouble and trial."[19] By *literal sense* Luther meant the plain meaning of the text. Mark Powell has suggested that this means, first and foremost, what the text would have meant to the original audience. As modern readers of the Bible, we get at the plain meaning of the text through asking the questions discussed in the Historical and Literary Readings. In truth, modern biblical interpretation was in some ways given birth by Luther when he put the Bible into the hands of all and encouraged educated study. These methods keep us grounded in history and in the rhetoric of the text itself. We might ask if our reading is free of artificial invention such as allegory. The overall question we bring is:

- What is the plain meaning of this text? Are we giving Scripture, in whatever ways we are able, its own integrity?

PUBLIC INTERPRETATION

Finally, for Lutherans, the interpretation of Scripture is a public act rather than a private one. The meaning of Scripture for individuals is to be found by seeking application of its universal message to personal situations. We do not believe that God speaks private messages to us through the Bible. So we might ask:

- Is the interpretation we are commending accessible to everyone? Are we gleaning lessons from the text that others might also hear and that we can explain?

One of the tricky aspects of understanding what is publicly accessible is that we are so easily bound by our own time and culture. Here we are often aided by listening to the voices from past traditions and voices from cultures other than our own. In this way the meaning of "public" is broadened, and our communities of reading are expanded beyond the confines of our particular group. We might ask:

- Are there interpretations from the past that help broaden and lend depth to our reading? Are there interpretations from cultures other than our own that might broaden or lend depth to our reading?

Each aspect of this Lutheran approach to studying the Bible is designed to make room for God's voice speaking to us through the Bible, beckoning us to lead lives worthy of our calling, laying out our sins, offering us God's grace, and delivering to us the promise that is ours in Christ.

Final Suggestions about How to Study the Bible

In this chapter we have explored four overlapping and interwoven ways we might open the Bible ourselves and begin to read and study. At a certain level the issues of which methods to use in biblical study and interpretation becomes a moot point. The crucial test is not whether certain tools are or are not used. The crucial test is whether the tools are used to further truthful and honest reading that frees the text to deepen faith and understanding, to spark faithful questions, to inspire works of justice and mercy, to speak law and gospel, and to drive us toward Christ. We are justified by faith, not by method!

Luther said "The Holy Scriptures require a humble reader who shows reverence and fear toward the Word of God, and constantly says, 'Teach me, teach me, teach me!' The Spirit resists the proud."[20]

So we bring to our study some overarching and guiding values.

We come to the Bible humbly, asking for the gift of faith and ever mindful of our own capacity for sin and self-deceit.

We come mindfully, bringing to our study the gifts of reason, the tools of scholarship, and the insights of others.

We come attentively, reading Scripture carefully and closely.

We come in the context of a faithful community, letting our stories interact with the stories of the Bible.

We come prayerfully, asking that the Holy Spirit might guide our study and that Christ might be among us.

And we come expectantly, listening for the voice of God working through the text and in the mutual study to inspire, shape, and enliven us individually and as a community of faith.

And so with these values as our guide, we invite you once again to open Scripture and join the conversation.

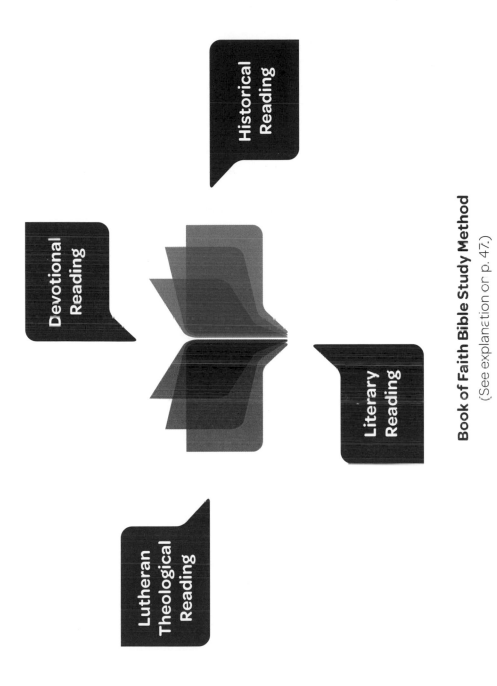

Historical Reading

Devotional Reading

Literary Reading

Lutheran Theological Reading

Book of Faith Bible Study Method
(See explanation or p. 47.)

4. Four Bible Studies

A Word about Method

There are many ways to approach studying the Bible. The following Bible studies will be presented using the four study methods introduced in chapter 3—Devotional, Literary, Historical, and Lutheran Theological. Any of the four study methods can be used as a way to encounter the Bible text, or all of them can be used together to have a fuller experience. Think of the methods as foundational stones. By stepping on each one you gain another perspective on the text. While these methods are not new, the specific emphasis on Lutheran theological insights is deliberate. You are encouraged to explore how these insights and interpretive principles can open up the Bible in a unique and helpful way.

While the studies share a common format, the way the methods are ordered vary in each study. This shows the flexible nature of these methods. One Bible text may lend itself to a particular method more naturally than another. For example, understanding a particular Bible text may depend heavily on understanding the historical context, so starting with questions of a historical nature may help unlock the meaning of the text, not only for the original hearers but also for us today.

All the methods take seriously the fact that adults are lifelong learners who come to a Bible study with a wealth of experience and a great deal to contribute. We are more likely to participate in Bible study that encourages us to draw upon our reservoir of experience and allows us to apply new knowledge and insights immediately to the specific contexts in our lives.[1] For example, a Bible study that begins with a Devotional method can provide a helpful focus and actively involve us in the learning process right from the start. But no matter where we begin, each method is intended to engage us in mind, emotion, and spirit as we explore questions and seek a renewed understanding of how God is at work in our lives and in the world.

Leading the Studies

It will be helpful for each study to be facilitated by one or more leaders. The role of a leader is important and involves advance preparation and planning. For example, the leader should read through the questions and, if necessary, do some advance research, especially on questions related to historic context. But these studies do not envision that the leader is the expert in the room. The leader is not expected to know or provide all the answers. In fact, the key role of the leader is to make room for the questions and encourage open discussion. The leader will find ways to invite adults to share their knowledge and experiences. These studies envision a learner- centered environment that will provide a safe setting for questions, with the leader encouraging adults to wonder and to be fully engaged, to revisit old understandings of the Word of God, and to imagine new understandings.

The following Bible studies will benefit from small group interaction. Talking in groups of two, three, or four can provide more opportunity for each person to share his or her thoughts or questions. Try small group conversations followed by reporting insights and questions back to the whole group. The studies are intended to provide an opportunity for you to get into the Bible with others. Sharing our conversations and our questions with others will help us discover how God may be speaking and what that may mean for our lives.

Study 1: Exodus 3:1-15
Diane Jacobson

Let's Begin with the Bible Text (5-10 minutes)

Each of the Bible studies in this book will begin with reading or "listening to" the Bible text. You may find it works well to have the text read aloud while others listen and *do not* follow along with the printed words. For this reading from Exodus 3, you may also consider three readers. The first voice would read the verses not in quotation marks and the second and third voice would speak the words in the quotation marks—one the voice of God (the Lord) and the other the voice of the Moses. It is always appropriate to begin a Bible study with prayer. This complete Bible study can be experienced in 50 to 90 minutes, depending on the amount of time you spend on each section. Leave some time at the end to summarize your experience together.

If the group wished to begin the session with a hymn, "How Firm a Foundation" (*ELW* 796) is a good option.

Exodus 3:1-15

[1]Moses was keeping the flock of his father-in-law Jethro, the priest of Midian; he led his flock beyond the wilderness, and came to Horeb, the mountain of God. [2]There the angel of the LORD appeared to him in a flame of fire out of a bush; he looked, and the bush was blazing, yet it was not consumed. [3]Then Moses said, "I must turn aside and look at this great sight, and see why the bush is not burned up." [4]When the LORD saw that he had turned aside to see, God called to him out of the bush, "Moses, Moses!" And he said, "Here I am." [5]Then he said, "Come no closer! Remove the sandals from your feet, for the place on which you are standing is holy ground." [6]He said further, "I am the God of your father, the God of Abraham, the God of Isaac, and the God of Jacob." And Moses hid his face, for he was afraid to look at God.

⁷Then the LORD said, "I have observed the misery of my people who are in Egypt; I have heard their cry on account of their taskmasters. Indeed, I know their sufferings, ⁸and I have come down to deliver them from the Egyptians, and to bring them up out of that land to a good and broad land, a land flowing with milk and honey, to the country of the Canaanites, the Hittites, the Amorites, the Perizzites, the Hivites, and the Jebusites. ⁹The cry of the Israelites has now come to me; I have also seen how the Egyptians oppress them. ¹⁰So come, I will send you to Pharaoh to bring my people, the Israelites, out of Egypt." ¹¹But Moses said to God, "Who am I that I should go to Pharaoh, and bring the Israelites out of Egypt?" ¹²He said, "I will be with you; and this shall be the sign for you that it is I who sent you: when you have brought the people out of Egypt, you shall worship God on this mountain."

¹³But Moses said to God, "If I come to the Israelites and say to them, 'The God of your ancestors has sent me to you,' and they ask me, 'What is his name?' what shall I say to them?" ¹⁴God said to Moses, "I AM WHO I AM." He said further, "Thus you shall say to the Israelites, 'I AM has sent me to you.'" ¹⁵God also said to Moses, "Thus you shall say to the Israelites, 'The LORD, the God of your ancestors, the God of Abraham, the God of Isaac, and the God of Jacob, has sent me to you': This is my name forever, and this my title for all generations."

Historical Reading (10-15 minutes)

The Book of Exodus tells the story of God saving Israel, the people God has personally claimed and promised to be with. In Exodus, God frees the people from the slavery in Egypt through the leadership of Moses (aided by his brother Aaron and sister Miriam). God leads the people across the sea to Mount Sinai where God makes a covenant with Israel and gives them the Ten Commandments and other laws. In this covenant, Israel is asked to respond to God's gift of saving them by becoming a nation dedicated to God, obeying God's voice and serving their neighbor.

Moses' encounter with God at the burning bush comes toward the beginning of the book of Exodus. Through this encounter God calls forth the leader who was needed for the task of delivering the Hebrew people out of slavery. This story is one of the first stories from the Bible many of us learn. We picture Moses in the desert, minding his own business, when suddenly faced with this dramatic sight, God calls to him and shakes up his world.

It may be helpful to set the stage for this story just a bit by looking at the historical context of the story. Start by noticing many of the names and places mentioned in the text.

- Who are Canaanites, the Hittites, the Amorites, the Perizzites, the Hivites, and the Jebusites?

The reality is that we are not exactly sure who some of these people are, and they have little real bearing on this particular story. Still, if you are curious you may find some background on these people by consulting a Bible dictionary.

- Who are the Egyptians and Israelites?
- Where is Midian? Where is Midian in relation to Egypt or Canaan?
- Why is Moses living in Midian?
- To which Pharaoh does this story refer?

Scholars speculate that the Egyptian king mentioned in Exodus 2:23 is Seti I. The pharaoh who followed him, and the one described in 3:10, may be Rameses II, who ruled from 1279-1212 BCE. He was most likely the Egyptian pharaoh at the time of the Israelite's exodus from Egypt. But notice that the Bible itself does not tell us these details because it is more interested in Moses and the Israelites and even Pharaoh's daughter than the great rulers of the day.

- Why are the Israelites living as slaves in Egypt?

Knowing the answers to all these questions may or may not help you discover the meaning of this text, but it can be useful to know the historical situation described. The first readers of this story would have been familiar with all these names and places, and they would have been a very important part of their "story." God acted to save the Israelite people in and through historic events. Though we cannot always know how much of each story is precise historical fact, we do know that the story of God's saving action in the Bible includes real people and places.

Sometimes, you can get answers to historical questions simply by reading more of the story. A quick review of Exodus, chapters 1 and 2, will answer some of the questions above. A good set of Bible maps (found in the back of many Bibles) will likely show locations mentioned in the story. Bible commentaries also give helpful background, but keep in mind that commentaries can also disagree over historical details because scholars are trying to piece together the context from very old sources. Asking historical questions can also lead you to notice other details in the story. For instance, why did God ask Moses to remove his sandals in 3:5? What traditions regarding sacred or holy places might have been influenced by this text?

- What other questions about the setting or context of the story do you have?

Devotional Reading (10-15 minutes)

One place to begin when reading and thinking about this story is to put yourself in Moses' shoes. Think about how Moses must have felt. Consider questions like these:

- How might you feel if you heard God speaking from a burning bush?
- Have you ever experienced what you might describe as a "call" from God?
- If you have never had such a dramatic "experience," has God called you anyway?
- How did Moses seem to feel about his leadership ability?
- Why might God call you? What are your leadership qualities?

- What does God promise to do for the Israelites (3:8)? How might you be "enslaved"? What would it mean to be free?
- What feelings do you have about what God asks and how Moses responds?

Using one of the other devotional methods described in chapter 3, you might also read the text using the Swedish marking method, marking:

a candle for a new idea;

a double candle for a verse to memorize;

an arrow for a verse that relates to personal experience;

and a question mark when something is not clear.

Then discuss your markings with others.

Literary Reading (10-20 minutes)

In the stories leading up to chapter 3 in Exodus, we find out many things about Moses—how he was born to a Hebrew family and put in a basket in the Nile River, where he was discovered and adopted by an Egyptian princess. Even though he grew up as part of the Egyptian royal family, Moses still identified with his enslaved people. He murdered a cruel Egyptian overseer and became an exile, marrying the daughter of a Midianite priest.

You learn a tremendous amount about the story in Exodus 3 if you read it very carefully, noticing some of the details, noticing some connections to other stories, and asking the literary questions you might put to any biblical narrative.

- For example, notice verse one. Moses' job is to lead his father-in-law's flock into the wilderness to the mountain of God. How is this similar to what God will call him to do later in the story?
- Now notice how the Mount Horeb is described. It is called "the mountain of God." So, something about the place Moses is leading the flock is sacred or holy. Again, how does this story seem to foreshadow what God is calling him to do for the Israelite people?

- Because the mountain in this story is called Horeb, many scholars who ask historical questions claim this story comes from a different tradition than the one that calls the mountain Sinai. But one very fascinating insight comes from looking closely at the Hebrew words of this text, which reveal just how closely linked these traditions are. The word for "bush" in Hebrew is *sineh*, which sounds a lot like *Sinai*. Moses' encounter with God in the flaming bush invites us to think about Israel's upcoming encounter with God at the fiery mountain (see Exodus 19:18). The call of the leader is closely tied to the call of the people.
- Another literary pattern that appears here and in other places in the Bible leads us to label this story as a "prophetic call" narrative. Notice what happens when God calls Moses' name. How does Moses respond? (3:4). God then commissions Moses for his particular task. Moses offers an objection to which God responds with assurance and a sign. Compare this to what happens when God calls Samuel (1 Samuel 3), Isaiah (Isaiah 6), Jeremiah (Jeremiah 1), or even Ananias (Acts 9). When we know what to look for when God calls a prophet, we notice the particular details of each call. Each call is individual and personal, much like our own. Moses and the others express their own feelings of inadequacy. Moses brings himself, with all his faults, to the encounter with God. God's sign to Moses is in the future, rather than the present. Moses takes on his task by depending entirely on the promise of God.
- How does hearing about or reading about how God has called others help you recognize your own "call narrative" (story)?
- A third literary detail of the text worth noticing is the relationship of seeing to hearing. Notice how many times these verbs appear. Moses *sees* the burning bush so that he might *hear* the call of God. Seeing serves hearing. God hears the cry of the people so that God might act. Hearing serves action. What other seeing and hearing is going on in this text? What do you make of these observations?
- A final literary detail worth noticing is how God's sacred name is revealed. Names are important in the Bible, particularly God's name.

God's name, *Yahweh*, might be translated "I am who I am," or perhaps "I will be who I will be." We want to know what God's name means, but perhaps the meaning is not so important as the reality of the name. The Ten Commandments tell us "You shall not make wrongful use of the name of the LORD your God" (Exodus 20:7). We might then ask: How could we make good use of God's name?

• Why does Moses want to know God's name? (3:13) Why do you think God's name is revealed in this text? How is this revelation of God's name related to what God intends to do for the people of Israel?

Lutheran Theological Reading (10-15 minutes)

Theological questions refer to questions that help us think about God and our relationship to God. They also call us into relationship with God. Here are some examples:

• What makes a place holy? What happens to Moses, to us, in sacred space?
• How did Moses react to God's call? How do we react?
• How do we hear God's call as a demand or as a promise? As both law and gospel? That is, when we hear God's call, do we feel inadequate? Empowered? Fearful? Energized? Scared? Upheld? What demands and promises do you hear in this passage?
• What is the relationship between the call in the text and God's mission to the world?
• How does this passage show forth Christ?
• How is the vocation of the leader tied to the vocation of the whole people of God?

Here are just a few implications of this story of the burning bush that result from asking the devotional, historical, literary, and Lutheran theological questions.

What makes this occasion holy is not some abstract standing on holy ground. The holy ground provides a context and a sign. The holy ground is a sign of God's presence, and it provides a context for the holy word that is to be spoken. Holy ground, sacred space, is where one pauses to find assurance—to give thanks, to worship, to learn—but it is a sending place, not an ending place. From the burning bush Moses looks out to the journey: to fleeing before Pharaoh, to crossing the sea, to arriving at the mountain, and finally to being brought into the Promised Land.

- Think of the way we Lutherans define the Word of God in three ways (see chapter 1)—as Jesus, the living Word; as the written Word in Scripture; and as the spoken or proclaimed word. Where do we hear holy words spoken? Why is such hearing and speaking so important?
- How are worship, Baptism, or even Bible study "sending places" and not simply ending places? How is God present in these places?

Moses' call is not his own. He is being called into God's mission to the world. God has seen Israel's suffering in slavery and intends to do something about it. God's character as a God who looks on suffering and is moved to respond, as one who keeps promises and acts to save, points us towards God's ultimate incarnation, death, and resurrection in Christ. Moses cannot alter God's character nor God's promise of freedom, but Moses can take up his call to become part of God's promise in action.

Being holy and being called are not private matters. Being made holy is not the equivalent of being more "spiritual." Moses' experience at the burning bush is not a private, spiritual cleansing. Seeing the miraculous creates space for hearing the call. Hearing then leads to action. The holy word given on holy ground is a vocational word, inviting us to take up our various calls in God's world and for God's world. This vocational calling is relational, invitational, and has outward purpose and direction. The word was not just for Moses; it was for Israel. And not just for Israel, but for the world.

The call of God is particular and personal. In the case of the burning bush, the word was particular to the context of Israel's enslavement and to the narrative of Moses' role within that context. The word is not an abstract, unchanging word given for all time. This is good news for us. This means that each encounter with the divine is new and personal with its own mission and content. We are not Moses, but our calling is also inescapably tied to God's mission in the world.

- To what mission are you called? To what mission is your congregation or institution called? How can this happen?

Finally, God's call to Moses is rooted in the promise of God's continuing presence. This promise is dynamic, rather than static; it is particular rather than abstract. God promises to be present with us even to the end of all the ages (see Matt 28:20). The Exodus encounter between Moses and God comes in the form of a flame. Like God's promise of continuing presence, this flame is available at all times. One encounters the flame when reading Scripture, when gathering in a community, when struggling with vocational direction. But be careful—fire can burn. Our encounters with God will not always be only comforting or inviting. We will all have objections and feelings of inadequacy or sin. In fact, that is how law functions—to reveal our sin, to show us that we are not whole without God. Fire burns and purifies. The encounter with the divine presence is likely to change our lives forever. But God will be present with us, lighting our way. This is God's gospel promise.

- How is God's Word like a flame? How does it function to burn and purify? How can "shedding light" on a subject function in both a positive and a negative way?
- As you consider your own "call story," what promise or good news do you hear in this story of Moses and the burning bush?

Before You Go (5-10 minutes)

No matter what method of Bible reading or study we may use, we are seeking to listen for how God is speaking in the text, and we are listening for how this word from God can renew, enliven, and empower our faith. Every time we read and study the Bible we listen for God's call in our lives. As you reflect on your experience today with this text and with these four Bible study methods, you may want to discuss one or more of the following questions:

How did you hear God speaking most clearly in the text?

What may God be calling you or us to do?

What did you like about this study?

What surprised you?

What are some of the benefits of each of the study methods?

How will your congregation be a Book of Faith congregation?

Closing Prayer

Almighty and eternal God, so draw our hearts to you, so guide our minds, so fill our imaginations, so control our wills, that we may be wholly yours, utterly dedicated to you; and then use us, we pray, as you will, but always to the glory and welfare of your people, through our Lord and Savior, Jesus Christ. Amen.

From Evangelical Lutheran Worship, page 86

Study 2: Jeremiah 1:4-19
Paul Lutz

Let's Begin with the Bible Text (5-10 minutes)

Again, you may wish to have this story read out loud while others listen and *do not* follow along with the printed words. If possible, three voices would be ideal for this reading. The first voice would read the verses not in quotation marks and the second and third voice would speak the words in the quotation marks—one the voice of God (the LORD) and the other the voice of the prophet (Jeremiah). If you are using the Devotional Method below, you may wish to read step one to participants prior to the reading of the text. It is always appropriate to begin a Bible study with prayer. This complete Bible study can be experienced in 50 to 90 minutes, depending on the amount of time you spend on each section. Leave some time at the end to summarize your experience together.

Jeremiah 1:4-19

[4]Now the word of the Lord came to me saying, [5]"Before I formed you in the womb I knew you, and before you were born I consecrated you; I appointed you a prophet to the nations." [6]Then I said, "Ah, Lord God! Truly I do not know how to speak, for I am only a boy." [7]But the Lord said to me, "Do not say, 'I am only a boy'; for you shall go to all to whom I send you, and you shall speak whatever I command you, [8]Do not be afraid of them, for I am with you to deliver you, says the Lord." [9]Then the Lord put out his hand and touched my mouth; and the Lord said to me, "Now I have put my words in your mouth. [10]See, today I appoint you over nations and over kingdoms, to pluck up and to pull down, to destroy and to overthrow, to build and to plant."

[11]The word of the Lord came to me, saying, "Jeremiah, what do you see?" And I said, "I see a branch of an almond tree." [12]Then the Lord said

to me, "You have seen well, for I am watching over my word to perform it." [13]The word of the Lord came to me a second time, saying, "What do you see?" And I said, "I see a boiling pot, tilted away from the north." [14]Then the Lord said to me: Out of the north disaster shall break out on all the inhabitants of the land. [15]For now I am calling all the tribes of the kingdoms of the north, says the Lord; and they shall come and all of them shall set their thrones at the entrance of the gates of Jerusalem, against all its surrounding walls and against all the cities of Judah. [16]And I will utter my judgments against them, for all their wickedness in forsaking me; they have made offerings to other gods, and worshiped the works of their own hands. [17]But you, gird up your loins; stand up and tell them everything that I command you. Do not break down before them, or I will break you before them. [18]And I for my part have made you today a fortified city, an iron pillar, and a bronze wall, against the whole land—against the kings of Judah, its princes, its priests, and the people of the land. [19]They will fight against you; but they shall not prevail against you, for I am with you, says the Lord, to deliver you.

Devotional Reading (10-20 minutes)

After listening to or reading through the Bible text, use the following four steps[2] and respond to the questions as you are inclined. Not all participants need to respond to any or all of the questions. All responses, however, should be received by the group without comment. Small groups of four or five provide the best opportunity for everyone to participate in discussions.

Step 1: Imagine the scene. Enter the story.

What do you see or notice in this story? What do you smell, touch, or feel?

Step 2: Find yourself in the scene. Reflect on relationships between characters in the story and your life situation.

How would you describe the relationship between Jeremiah and the Lord? Explain.

Step 3: Connect some element of this biblical story with your own life experience.

What would you say is the "good news" in this narrative? In what way is it good news?

79

Step 4: Act on your insights. Plan a specific response, whether large or small. Let the words become flesh in your own life.

If you were to name this story, give it a title, what would it be? Explain.

Literary Reading (10-20 minutes)

A text can be understood by focusing on the text itself, its literary features, its artistry, the *way* it makes its point. Attention to the text itself can be a key to understanding the meaning of the text. A Literary Guide can be helpful in finding new and rich insights from the Bible. The Bible study leader may wish to have a sample of several literary guides available for the participants to use. In addition, Bibles used should be reliable translations and not a paraphrase. Also, Bibles will be most useful if they are annotated, that is, if they have notes that give information on related Bible verses, possible translations of difficult words or phrases, and details useful for understanding the verses you are studying.

You are encouraged to respond to the following questions. Again, not everyone needs to respond to every question, and agreement in responses between participants is not necessary. Select whatever questions are of most interest to you.

1. *Identify the type of writing.*
- What is the literary form of this story?
- Is this story to be taken literally or figuratively? Why do you think so?
- If you were to use a phrase to explain what is happening in this text, what would it be?
- Compare what is happening in this text to Jeremiah to what happened to Moses in Exodus 3:1-15 (see study 1, pp. 68-77). How are these stories similar or different?

2. *Search the original meaning. Study the words, symbols, and images to understand what the writer may have intended.*
- How do you think the first hearers understood the story? How might they have understood the two symbolic visions?

- What would they have made of the fact that in Hebrew the words for *watching* and *almond tree* sound similar?

Historical Reading (10-20 minutes)

When studying the Bible it is helpful not only to consider the written words but also the historical and cultural contexts of the text. A text can be understood to reflect its author, the circumstances being addressed by the author, and the author's audience. Knowing something about the author of a biblical text and the setting in which it was written can be a key to understanding the meaning of the text. For example, notice how much historical information is given in the first three verses of the book of Jeremiah. Jeremiah is a prophet in the southern kingdom of Judah, and Josiah, a relatively good and faithful king, is ruling. But Jeremiah also prophesied under the rule of Johoiakim and Zedekiah, two rulers who were not strong protectors of the faith. In fact, Zedekiah was the last king of Judah prior to the armies of Babylon destroying Jerusalem and carrying away many of the people of Judah into captivity in Babylonia. It was a very challenging time to be a prophet and speak God's words of judgment.

Being God's prophet in the late seventh and early sixth centuries before Christ obliged Jeremiah to speak God's truth in a time of vast historical changes. These changes included the realignment of power among the empires adjacent to Jeremiah's small kingdom of Judah, as well as sweeping reforms within the entire country. In these opening verses, we hear how the Lord placed three visions before Jeremiah. The first vision was an almond branch from the first of the trees that flowers in the spring. This was a sign the Lord was watching to ensure that as spring comes forth, so will God's word come forth. The vision of the boiling pot tilted away from the north declares the impending destruction on Jerusalem and summarized the divine message that would dominate Jeremiah's preaching: the coming judgment of God against the wickedness of the people of Judah who were forsaking God by sacrificing "to strange gods" (1:16). The last vision concerned Jeremiah's own person: God would make him "a fortified city, an iron pillar, and a bronze wall, against the whole land" (vs. 18), even if the people of Judah should fight him, for the Lord solemnly promised that "they shall not prevail against you, for I am with you, says the Lord, to deliver you" (vs. 19).

Many different kinds of study tools are available to assist readers in engaging the historical world of the Bible. Some of these tools are Bible dictionaries, Bible atlases, Bible commentaries, and Bible concordances. The Bible study leader may wish to have samples of these tools available for the participants to use.

The Historical approach involves the following steps of study. You are encouraged to respond to the following questions. Again, not everyone needs to respond to every question and agreement in responses between participants is not necessary.

Describe the historical situation. Use a Bible dictionary or Bible commentary to get clues. Select whatever questions are of most interest to the participants.

Who is speaking? Who is the audience?

What is the situation for the writer? What is the occasion?

What is the intention of the passage?

What historical situation lies behind the passage? For example, who are the tribes of the kingdoms of the north?

How would you define the authority and extent of Jeremiah's call?

How does knowing something of the historical situation influence our understanding of these verses from Jeremiah?

Lutheran Theological (10-20 minutes)

Here are three Lutheran insights concerning Biblical interpretation methods.

We study the Bible listening for law and gospel. As we study certain passages, we may hear God's judgments for the world and us. This is called the law. We experience the law when we are confronted with our sin. As we study other passages, we may hear God's love, grace, and promises for the world and us. That is called the gospel. We experience the gospel when we are overwhelmed by God's grace.

We study the Bible with the Bible. The best resource for Bible study is the Bible. A panoramic view of the biblical story can provide balance for difficult passages, stories, and themes. To ignore the whole biblical story is to run the risk of taking passages out of context and reducing the Bible to a collection of moral laws or a holy rule book. Scripture must be used to interpret Scripture.

We study the Bible in light of justification by grace. We are saved by God's grace through faith in Jesus, not by how we feel, or having the right experience, or what we accomplish. Because of Christ, all are accepted into the community of God's people. The central message of the Bible is both simple and yet grand. God loves us, forgives us, and makes us the church.

With these insights in mind, explore some or all of the following questions:

How do these Lutheran insights help in the interpretation of this passage?

What similarities could you list between God's calling, supporting, and sending of Jeremiah and God's calling, supporting, and sending of you?

This text is the first reading for the Fourth Sunday in Epiphany (year C). The Gospel reading is Luke 4:21-30. Read this passage. How does this influence your reading and interpretation of the Jeremiah text?

What in this text seems to be "law," God's word of judgment? Where do you see "gospel," God's message of promise?

Compare this text with similar texts. How does the call narrative in Jeremiah compare to other prophetic calls, such as in Exodus 3:1-4:17; Isaiah 6:1-13; Ezekiel 2:1-3:15; or Galatians 1:15-16? What are some of the similarities, differences? If Jeremiah's call is similar to other call narratives, what does that suggest about how we might understand the text?

So what? What difference does it make that God spoke and acted in that situation with Jeremiah? What does it have to do with you (us) or say to you (us) today?

What other Lutheran insights might you suggest be applied for a clearer understanding of this text?

Before You Go (5-10 minutes)

No matter what method of Bible reading or study we may use, we are seeking to listen for how God is speaking in the text, and we are listening for how this word from God can renew, enliven, and empower our faith. Like

Jeremiah, every time we read and study the Bible we listen for God's call in our lives. As you reflect on your experience today with this text and with these four Bible study methods, share with others:

How did you hear God speaking most clearly in the text?

What may God be calling you or us to do?

What did you like about this study?

What surprised you?

Where or how do you imagine these methods could be used in your congregation? What will you do to make that happen?

How will your congregation encourage members of all ages to be engaged with the Bible?

Closing Prayer

Blessed Lord God, you have caused the Holy Scriptures to be written for the nourishment of your people. Grant that we may hear them, read, mark, learn, and inwardly digest them, that, comforted by your promise, we may embrace and forever hold fast to the hope of eternal life, which you have given us in Jesus Christ, our Savior and Lord. Amen.

—*From Evangelical Lutheran Worship, page 72*

Study 3: John 8:31-36
Kathryn Kleinhans

Let's Begin with the Bible Text (5-10 minutes)

John 8:31-36 is the Gospel text appointed for Reformation Sunday. In keeping with the spirit of the Reformation, the opening and closing prayers are selected from Martin Luther's writings. You might also wish to consider reading or singing one of these hymns before you begin your study: "Thy Strong Word," *ELW* 511, or "Lord, Keep Us Steadfast in Your Word," *ELW* 517.

Opening Prayer

Eternal God and Father of our Lord Jesus Christ,
give us your Holy Spirit who writes the preached word into our hearts.
May we receive it and believe it and be cheered and comforted by it
   in eternity.
Glorify your word in our hearts
and make it so bright and warm that we may find pleasure in it,
through your Holy Spirit think what is right,
and by your power fulfill the word,
for the sake of Jesus Christ, your Son, our Lord. Amen.
   —From Martin Luther, Luther's Prayers, *ed. Herbert F. Brokering*
   (Minneapolis: Augsburg, 1967), 65-66

John 8:31-36

[31]Then Jesus said to the Jews who had believed in him, "If you continue in my word, you are truly my disciples; [32]and you will know the truth, and the truth will make you free." [33]They answered him, "We are descendants of Abraham and have never been slaves to anyone. What do you mean by saying, 'You will be made free'?" [34]Jesus answered them, "Very

truly, I tell you, everyone who commits sin is a slave to sin. [35]The slave does not have a permanent place in the household; the son has a place there forever. [36]So if the Son makes you free, you will be free indeed."

Historical Reading (10-20 minutes)

John's Gospel is the last of the four canonical Gospels to be written. It was most likely written in the 90s, since it reflects growing tensions (and eventual separation) between Jewish Christians and the rest of the Jewish community following the destruction of the Jerusalem temple by the Romans in 70 CE.

New Testament scholars think that the Gospel of John, the three letters of John, and Revelation were not written by the beloved disciple himself but by members of a "Johannine community" of Christians, perhaps founded by the beloved disciple, located in Asia Minor near Ephesus. The Gospel's witness to Jesus is shaped by the context of this particular late first-century Christian community. In addition to the tensions with the Jewish community, the Gospel reflects internal concerns about authority and leadership within the Johannine community as the generation of those who knew Jesus and his disciples firsthand dies out.

Being attentive to the differences between the historical context of the Gospel writer and our own historical context will help us both to understand the text in its own right and to apply it to our lives today.

In this text, the Jews say that they "have never been slaves to anyone." But the Israelites *were* slaves in Egypt before the Exodus! Later, in the sixth century BCE, many of the Jewish people were captured and deported to Babylon. In Jesus' own time, Palestine had been under Roman rule for a century.

- Why do you think they say that they have never been in bondage? Have they forgotten their history? Are they in a state of denial? Are they implying that they have maintained their spiritual freedom despite physical and political bondage?
- What difference does it make, if any, in how you understand their conversation with Jesus?

The Gospel of John reflects first-century tensions between Jewish Christians (Jews who accepted Jesus as God's Messiah) and the Jewish community as a whole. Passages such as John 9:13-22; 12:42; and 16:1-4 express the concern that Jewish Christians will be expelled from the synagogues. This is one example of how the situation of the later Johannine community is projected into the Gospel narrative of Jesus' earthly ministry.

John 7-8 shows Jesus teaching in the Jerusalem temple. In this passage, Jesus raises the question of whether or not the Jews who had come to believe in him would "continue" in his word. What factors might have kept them from continuing in Jesus' word? What are today's challenges, for us, to continuing in the word?

There is a long history of Christian anti-Semitism, in which Christians blamed—and persecuted—Jewish people as "Christ-killers." Some Christian groups, including the ELCA, have apologized for this history. How might our sensitivity to this injustice shape the way we read this text today?

We who live in North America enjoy political freedoms that come with democracy. In spite of this, what captivities might Jesus challenge us to recognize in ourselves? If your Bible study group includes descendants of slaves or Christians from countries in Africa, Asia, Latin America, or Eastern Europe, where freedom struggles are more recent (and even still ongoing), invite them to share their insights into this text.

Lutheran Theological Reading (10-20 minutes)

It's interesting to note that the Gospel of John was Martin Luther's favorite Gospel because of its strong focus on Christ.

- Why do you think John 8:31-36 is the Gospel text appointed for Reformation Sunday?

In the ELCA Confession of Faith, we acknowledge "the Word of God" in three forms: Jesus Christ as the incarnate Word, the proclamation of God's message of Law and Gospel as the preached word, and the inspired canonical scriptures as the written word. How does this three-fold understanding of the Word of God shape your understanding of what Jesus means when he talks about continuing in his word?

Martin Luther and subsequent Lutheran theology distinguish between two ways in which we experience God's Word: Law, which functions as a command, telling us what to do, and Gospel, which functions as a promise, offering us what God in Christ has already done for us. The Lutheran confessional writings insist that "the law always accuses us." Only the Gospel brings us into right relationship with God—by grace, through faith.

The medical profession gives us a helpful model for understanding the relationship between Law and Gospel: diagnosis and prognosis. We can approach any scriptural passage fruitfully by asking two questions:

- What is the diagnosis of the human condition—and of the church—in this text?
- What is the prognosis for the human condition—and for the church—in this text?

The human situation is complex. Just as a physician needs to look beyond the presenting symptoms to discover the root cause of the sickness, the reader of the Scriptures needs to probe the surface problems in the text to reach the "God-sized" problem. How does a particular text present the human condition not just as an unpleasant illness but as a terminal disease that can only be remedied by the saving death of Christ? And how does the text show us an alternative future for those who are in Christ, as not only resurrection to new life after death but also resurrection to a new life bearing fruit in the here and now?

In John 8:31-36, Jesus' diagnoses the human problem as bondage, not just physical and political bondage but bondage to sin itself. Given this diagnosis, what's the prognosis? When the Son makes us free and gives us a place in the household, what, concretely, does that look like for Christians and Christian communities today?

The text also presents the problem of unbelief: Will those who initially believed in Jesus *continue* in his word? Or will they run away from (or even be evicted from!) the household of faith? When the diagnosis is unbelief, what is the prognosis? What does belief look like, and how does it bear fruit for those who are adopted into Christ's family?

Vocation, the Christian calling to serve the neighbor for Christ's sake is another central Lutheran theme. In John 8:31-36, Jesus speaks explicitly of freedom from slavery to sin. What does your study of this text suggest that we might be freed for?

Literary Reading (10-20 minutes)

From its very beginning and throughout, the way the Gospel of John is written differs from the other three Gospels. Noting these differences and the particular way they express the meaning of Christ reveals much about the unique purpose of this particular Gospel, which is summed up in John 20:30-31. Here are some other ways to explore the unique message of John:

If you can, set aside an uninterrupted period of time to read through the entire Gospel of John. As you read, pay particular attention to the occurrences of "word" and "truth," which are important literary motifs in John's Gospel. Are there other repeated words, images, or themes in John's Gospel that catch your attention?

Read John 1:1-18 and John 14:1-7. Instead of a birth narrative, John's Gospel begins with a poetic passage describing how the Word of God "became flesh and dwelt among us, full of grace and truth." In John 14:6, Jesus identifies himself as "the way, the truth, and the life." How might these two passages deepen your understanding of Jesus' words in John 8:31-32?

Read John 14:15-21; 15:26-27; and 16:12-15. John 14:1-16:33 is called Jesus' Farewell Discourse, spoken at his last meal with his disciples. In the selected verses, Jesus describes the role of "the Spirit of truth" whom he will send to them. What is the relationship between Jesus who is the truth (John 14:6) and "the Spirit of truth"? Does thinking about the Holy Spirit as "the Spirit of truth" add new insight to your understanding of John 8:31-36?

In a courtroom, witnesses take an oath to tell "the truth, the whole truth, and nothing but the truth." Read John 18:37-38. How does your understanding of "truth" in John's Gospel shape your own self-understanding as one called to witness to Jesus Christ? How would you respond to the people you encounter today who ask "What is truth?" Passages such as John 19:35; 20:30-31; and 21:24-25 highlight the evangelist as a trustworthy witness to Jesus, so that others may come to believe in him. What would your congregation need to do to be recognized by non-members as a trustworthy witness to Jesus?

Usually, we think of truth as an object, grammatically speaking. We find out the truth. We tell the truth. But in John 8:32, truth also functions as the subject of the verb: "the truth will make you free." How can the truth make us free? Is there a difference between verse 32 ("the truth will make you free") and verse 36 ("the Son makes you free")?

Devotional Reading (10-20 minutes)

Have someone in the group read John 8:31-36 aloud. As you listen, pay attention to the words that strike you or the images that arise. With one or two others, discuss your impressions. What was meaningful for you, and why? Did hearing the text, rather than reading it, give you any new insights?

Jesus uses a family metaphor ("a permanent place in the household") to contrast Christian freedom with slavery to sin. Have someone in the group read the text aloud for a second time. As you listen, hold in mind your experiences of family. Pray silently for the members of your family and others who are close to you. Then pray silently, or ask a member of the group to say a prayer out loud, for "the family of faith" (both your local congregation and the wider church).

In Genesis, Abraham is blessed so that he and his family may be a blessing to the world. If being descendants of Abraham means being a blessing to others, in what ways are *we* such a blessing today?

Have someone in the group read John 8:31-36 aloud for a third time. As you listen, can you think of one specific thing you might do as a response to your new understanding of this passage?

Before You Go (5-10 minutes)

Take a moment to reflect on your time together by answering one or more of the following questions:

- How did you hear God speaking most clearly in the text?
- What may God be calling you or us to do?
- What did you like about this study?
- What surprised you?
- How will your congregation encourage members of all ages to be engaged with the Bible?

Closing Prayer

O Father of all mercy, you have begun your work in us.
Continue to fill us with all dimensions of wisdom and knowledge.
May we be fully certain in our heart
and fully aware how the Spirit, who has raised up our Lord,
also enlivens the faith within us with the same power and strength.
Through him we have also risen from the dead by his mighty power,
which works in us through your holy word.
Help us to grow in the knowledge of your dear Son,
   our Lord Jesus Christ,
and to remain firm in confessing his blessed word.
Give us the grace to be agreed in mind and to serve one another
   in Christ.
Amen
   —From Martin Luther, Luther's Prayers, ed. Herbert F. Brokering
   (Minneapolis: Augsburg, 1967), 66.

Study 4: Romans 7:15-25a
R. Guy Erwin

Let's Begin with the Bible Text (5-10 minutes)

This dramatic text from Romans 7 (which appears in Lectionary 14 of Year A) is a somewhat mysterious transitional passage taken from Paul's discussion of the implications of Christ's death and resurrection in the middle part of his letter to the Romans. Many scholars have tried to interpret this passage, but none have ever done so definitively—there has always remained a little uncertainty about exactly what Paul was trying to say here—and now you, reader, have the opportunity to wrestle with it too. All of the ways previously suggested to you in this book as good paths on which to approach Bible texts apply very well to this particular passage, and as you use them, they may take you to some unexpected places and raise some new questions you didn't anticipate. Read the text through once. Pause and reflect on parts that are difficult to understand. Then read it again. Whether you are studying this text alone or as part of a group, be sure to allow time to reflect on each section, and a chance to do some overall thinking at the end.

Romans 7:15-25a

[15]I do not understand my own actions. For I do not do what I want, but I do the very thing I hate. [16]Now if I do what I do not want, I agree that the law is good. [17]But in fact it is no longer I that do it, but sin that dwells within me. [18]For I know that nothing good dwells within me, that is, in my flesh. I can will what is right, but I cannot do it. [19]For I do not do the good I want, but the evil I do not want is what I do. [20]Now if I do what I do not want, it is no longer I that do it, but sin that dwells within me.

[21]So I find it to be a law that when I want to do what is good, evil lies close at hand. [22]For I delight in the law of God in my inmost self, [23]but I

see in my members another law at war with the law of my mind, making me captive to the law of sin that dwells in my members. [24]Wretched man that I am! Who will rescue me from this body of death? [25]Thanks be to God through Jesus Christ our Lord!

Historical Reading (10-20 minutes)

First, let's ask the basic question we always start with when we approach a Biblical text: What's Paul writing about? For this, we need the wider context of the verses on either side of this section. If we were to go back to the previous chapter (chapter 6), we would find that Paul began with a general discussion of what it means to "live in Christ" through God's grace. Then, at the end of chapter 6 and into chapter 7, Paul turns to the question most on his mind: if salvation comes to us by grace through faith, how should we now regard God's law? What does it mean to a believer? This was a particularly important question for those whose whole understanding of religious faithfulness and meaning came from obedience to divine laws. How were they now suddenly to reinterpret what it meant to be a believer, when the principal way of being one was to be a follower of the law?

But the question is even broader than that, and still relevant to us almost two millennia later: How does our salvation by God's mercy and grace relate to our struggle to live good and moral lives? How are these things connected? This is the framework within which our text selection fits.

In verses 1 through 14 of chapter 7, Paul explains that the law that regulates the lives of humans pertains only to their bodies, so that to live in Christ (which Paul calls having "died to the law" through Christ) is to live in freedom from the law. But what does Paul mean by "law" here? He makes a distinction between our living "in the flesh"—by which he means in a way ruled by our feelings and desires—and living the "new life of the Spirit." The purpose the law serves is to awaken in a person the sense of sinfulness. As Paul sees it, humans will always resist the law, and so the law will provoke rebellion in them. The result is that where there is knowledge of the law there is knowledge of sin, which Paul understands as the beginning of a person's understanding of the need for God's grace and mercy. The law is good because it "lays bare human rebelliousness." And it is good because knowing one's sin then leads to depending on God. So far, so good (or not good, as the case may be).

Now, in verse 15, Paul changes gears a bit, and talks about himself as a living example of this complicated and paradoxical truth about humankind. Again and again in this section, Paul uses the pronoun "I," something he has not done before in regard to sin and grace—earlier it was always "we" and "us"—but now it's getting personal, both for Paul and for his audience. He wants his readers and listeners to know that he understands this truth about sin and law not as something theoretical or abstract, but right there in his own heart and mind and life. But what does it have to do with us and our experience?

Paul is writing to a faraway group of believers to help them understand what it means to believe in Jesus, and what implications that believing has for their religious life. Whether Jews or Gentiles, much of what they have understood up to now about God's expectations for them has revolved around two things: correct worship and moral behavior. How might this text challenge them?

As you think about this text in this way, ask yourself these questions:

- What kind of message is Paul sending in this text?
- Is it teaching, preaching, correcting, or consoling? Or something else?
- Who is Paul's audience?
- What does he want them to think?
- Do the words sound the same to you as you think they would have sounded to first-century Romans?
- How might these words have sounded to Christians who had been brought up in the Jewish faith and its observance of law as faithful response to God?

Literary Reading (10-20 minutes)

This brings us to our second basic question: Is there something significant about the particular form or style of this piece of text? In this case there must be—look at how Paul has changed so dramatically to the first person singular: "I," he insists, "it is I who does these things." Is this just his vivid description of his personal experience? Probably not. He may well think that the "I" of the writer will speak directly to the heart of the "I" who is the reader—in fact, you.

- When Paul writes, "I," can you also identify with what he is saying? Is it possible that you could even say the same thing about your own experiences?

For some of us, Paul's admission of confusion may be reassuring. If even Saint Paul can be confused, maybe it's OK if I am confused sometimes too. That seems to be what Paul wants us to think—that the experience he describes is one that we will understand and be able to empathize with, because, in fact, we probably share it.

- How do you feel about the gap between what you want and what you think you ought to want? Do you sort your "wants" into categories of "good" and "bad"? Do you feel a tension here? How does this tension affect the way you feel about God?
- Or is it for you not so much a case of wanting things you think you shouldn't want, as it is a gap between what you want and what you can have? Do your desires always greatly outstrip your abilities or opportunities? There is tension in that as well—the gap between what "is" and what you "wish there was." How does this tension feel? How does it make you feel about God?

Both of these are situations of frustration and longing and guilt, whether you desire what you think or know is wrong, or simply want more than you can reasonably have or need. Such desire, as Paul understands it, draws the heart away from God and makes it rebellious and defiant. And the case he knows best is his very own.

Paul describes a situation that is not as it should be: "I do this, but I should do that." "But" is the key word here—things are not as they should be. What Paul does is contrary to his desires on one level, but he does it anyway. There is tension in this: something is that shouldn't be. How can this tension be resolved? Clearly, Paul is uncomfortable with it.

As you think about this text in this way, ask yourself these questions:

- What is the "shape" of this passage?
- Is it complete in itself, or does it seem fragmentary?
- What is the form of address? Who is speaking and who is spoken to?
- What words recur again and again?
- What patterns are visible in Paul's choice of language?
- Does the text lead up to a specific ending? If so, what is the conclusion or climax of this section of Paul's letter?

Lutheran Theological Reading (10-20 minutes)

Many Lutherans, when they hear the word "law" in a text like this, (especially one that expresses some tension with the law being described, as it does here) think right away about "law and gospel," one of the main lenses with which we look at Scripture. Does that concept apply here? Is the tension in this passage between "law" and "grace" or between "law" and "sin"?

When we Lutherans speak of "law," we don't just mean laws or rules and regulations—or at least not those things alone. We also don't mean just God's Law as the Bible communicates it in the religious laws of the people of Israel enshrined in the Torah—those laws that begin with the Ten Commandments and descend down to the many specific laws of food, worship, and behavior that gave the people's lives structure and gave them a sense of connectedness to God.

What we Lutherans mean by "law" in this bigger theological sense is different, and much less literal: it means all the things inside and outside us that tend to draw us away from a sense of God's mercy and love for us, and instead lead us toward fear and despair and hopelessness. In this passage it is this more abstract understanding of law that Paul identifies with "flesh"—his bodily existence and the way his body governs even his mind.

Paul is no simple dualist here, opposing the body on the one side to the soul on the other, but he is one who understands that in human life the two parts are always intimately connected. We live in and with both at the same time, even when they are sometimes at odds with each other: in our "inmost self" we delight in the law of God, and at the same time we see "in our members" a captivity to the law of sin. For Paul, the language of "flesh" and "spirit" are metaphors for what draws us away from God and what pulls us toward God, whether physical, emotional, or mental. It is not our embodiedness in itself, but our spiritual rebelliousness that is at issue.

There is another powerful Lutheran idea revealed in this as well: the condition of the believer as a person caught between righteousness and sinfulness, at the same time righteous (through God's grace) and sinful (in the limitations of human desire and selfishness). Luther called this being a "saint and sinner at the same time," and he believed it explained much about human nature and the complexity of human reactions even to God. Paul seems here to be speaking of much the same thing, a sense of being suspended between God and sin. It's not a comfortable place to be, caught in the middle of opposing impulses, but Paul is making the point that we have no choice—that our wills are not strong enough to break us free from our human limitations, but we keep trying, even as we know that our salvation comes from God and not our own striving or achieving.

Perhaps this is what Paul means when he speaks of his wretchedness and this captivity in a "body of death": that viewed from an exclusively human perspective, life is frustrating and short and futile—but seen in the light of Christ and lived in the grace of God, even the struggle to live an unselfish life gains meaning and is no longer useless, self-defeating effort but can actually mean something worthwhile.

As you think about this text in this way, ask yourself these questions:

- Does this text make sense in light of these Lutheran principles of "law and gospel" and "saved and yet a sinner"? If so, how?
- Does this reflect what you understand to be the main message of Scripture?
- How do the categories described (law/gospel; saint/sinner) help you make sense of your life and your experience of humans?
- How do these categories open up this text to new understandings?

Devotional Reading (10-20 minutes)

"Who will rescue me?" Paul asks, and answers himself simply with a declaration: "Thanks be to God through Jesus Christ our Lord!" With this Paul returns to the theme with which he began this section of Romans: that it is in Jesus' death and resurrection that Christians die to sin and rise to eternal life.

This text is complex and many-layered, and a bit self-contradictory in places—not an easy nut to crack. And many have discussed and debated it before us and will again. But it also speaks to us in the here and now, and in its intensity and realism about human frailty, it has something to say to each believer.

How does it touch you? Is Paul's language of frustration with his own contrary desires something with which you can identify? Paul doesn't leave us (at least in this passage) with much in the way of instructions as to how to apply these ideas to ourselves in a useful and productive way.

But there is a devotional message here too. We could describe it as being a tough but clear-eyed look at human pride and willfulness balanced with a strong sense of God's power to overcome even human resistance through the gospel of Jesus Christ. In some ways this is a text well suited to penitential or self-critical reflection, since it focuses extensively on self-doubt and the sense of being trapped in rebellion against God. But it ends on a liberating note, and it comes out of a letter whose whole message is one of forgiveness and grace. There is hope beyond the self-doubt—hope in One whose power is even greater than that of endless human self-centeredness. And for that: "Thanks be to God through Jesus Christ our Lord!"

As you think about this text in this way, ask yourself these questions:

- Are you, like Paul, caught in a struggle with yourself over doing what is right?
- Have you ever felt frustration with your inability to control your thoughts and feelings?
- How do you cope with the contradictions you find within your own heart?
- As you read this text, what prayers of repentance or thankfulness come to mind?
- Is "Who will rescue me?" one of your questions, too? If so, what is your answer?
- How does this text make you feel about God's love for you?

Before You Go (5-10 minutes)

Take a moment to think or talk about how this text has made you feel. Have you gained a better sense of what Paul means to communicate in this passage? Does it speak to you where you are? How has it made you think about yourself as a child of God and an heir of Christ? How have you grown by this study? How would you express what you have learned to someone else?

Closing Prayer

> You are great, O God, and greatly to be praised. You have made us for yourself, and our hearts are restless until they rest in you. Grant that we may believe in you, call upon you, know you, and serve you, through your Son, Jesus Christ, our Savior and Lord. Amen.
> —From Evangelical Lutheran Worship, page 41.

Endnotes

1. God's Powerful Book

1. Henry Offermann, quoted in Erik Heen, "The Bible among Lutherans in America: The ELCA as a Test Case," *Dialog: A Journal of Theology* 45 (Spring 2006): 9. Heen favorably quotes this 1930s statement of his predecessor in the New Testament department at The Lutheran Theological Seminary at Philadelphia. Heen concludes his article by affirming for a new century the urgent imperative to "state *anew*" our Lutheran, Christocentric perspective on the Bible, op. cit., 19.

2. Wolfhart Pannenberg, *Systematic Theology*, vol. 2, trans. Geoffrey Bromiley (Grand Rapids, Mich.: Eerdmans, 1994), 463.

3. From *Constitutions, Bylaws and Continuing Resolutions of the Evangelical Lutheran Church in America®*, 19.

4. All good literature does this to some extent, as W. H. Auden says in his poem "Words:" "A sentence uttered makes a world appear. . . ."

5. Darrell Jodock, *The Church's Bible: Its Contemporary Authority* (Minneapolis: Augsburg Fortress, 1989), 143.

6. Karlfried Froehlich, in Terrence E. Fretheim and Karlfried Froehlich, *The Bible as Word of God in a Postmodern Age* (Minneapolis: Fortress Press, 1998), 45.

7. "Confession of Faith," *The Constitution of the Evangelical Lutheran Church in America*, 2.03. This ELCA provision draws on long-standing Lutheran convictions stated in the 1570s in the opening paragraphs of the Formula of Concord, one of the primary Lutheran statements of faith:

> We believe, teach, and confess that the only rule and guiding principle according to which all teachings and teachers are to be evaluated and judged are the prophetic and apostolic writings of the Old and New Testaments alone, as it is written, "Your word is a lamp to my feet and a light to my path" (Ps. 119[:105]), and Saint Paul: "If . . . an angel from heaven should proclaim to you something contrary, . . . let that one be accursed!" (Gal. 1[:8]).

(Robert Kolb, and Timothy J. Wengert, eds., *The Book of Concord: The Confessions of the Evangelical Lutheran Church* [Minneapolis: Augsburg Fortress, 2000], 486.)

8. *The Use of the Means of Grace: A Statement on the Practice of Word and Sacrament* (Evangelical Lutheran Church in America, 1997), 12. Adopted for guidance and practice by the Fifth Biennial Churchwide Assembly of the Evangelical Lutheran Church in America, August 19, 1997.

9. "Holy Baptism," *Evangelical Lutheran Worship* (Minneapolis: Augsburg Fortress, 2006), 228.

10. "Affirmation of Baptism," *Evangelical Lutheran Worship*, 236.

11. Karlfried Froehlich, *The Bible as Word of God in a Postmodern Age*, 132.

12. Kathryn A. Kleinhans, "The Word Made Words: A Lutheran Perspective on the Authority and Use of the Scriptures," *Word & World: Theology for Christian Ministry* 26/4 (Fall 2006): 409.

13. For further reading on the authority of the Bible for Lutherans, there are many recent essay collections including *Word & World* 26/4 (Fall 2006); *Dialog: A Journal of Theology* 45 (Spring 2006); David C. Ratke, ed., *Hearing the Word: Lutheran Hermeneutics, A Vision of Life Under the Gospel* (Minneapolis: Lutheran University Press, 2006), which publishes presentations from the 2005 convocation of the Association of Teaching Theologians-ELCA; and Reinhard Boettcher, ed., *Witnessing to God's Faithfulness: Issues of Biblical Authority* (The Lutheran World Federation, 2006), which records a global conversation.

14. The Book of Faith Initiative in the ELCA was developed in response to a proposal from the North Carolina Synod and approved by the 2007 Churchwide Assembly. To learn more and be part of this initiative, visit www.elca.org/bookoffaith.

3. How Can the Bible Be Studied?

1. The method or approach called "Historical" in this book is also known especially in academic study as the Historical-Critical approach. The "critical" is not about criticizing but rather about various study disciplines such as text criticism and form criticism. In these technical disciplines,

ancient texts are studied to observe differences and develop theories about how the texts were formed. In our studies, the attention will primarily be on the historic context and the people, places, events, and objects that are part of the biblical record and world of the Bible.

2. The Literary Reading approach also includes the related category of rhetorical study of the text.

3. These four methods will serve as the underlying methodology of an adult Bible study that will be available in Spring 2009. Training events will be held at a variety of sites in places served by the ELCA.

4. Many people have written about the *Lectio Divina*. See particularly Fr. Luke Dysinger, O.S.B., *Accepting The Embrace of God: The Ancient Art of Lectio Divina* , 1990 (www.valyermo.com/ld-art.html) and Lisa Dahill, *Truly Present* (Minneapolis: Augsburg Fortress, 2005), 67-72.

5. Ibid.

6. The T.R.I.P. method is featured in the yearly publication *Daily Texts: Bible Verses and Prayers for Each Day of the Year* (Alexandria, Minn.: Mount Carmel Ministries). See www.dailytext.com.

7. Mark Allan Powell, *How Lutherans Interpret the Bible*, DVD series (Columbus, OH: Select Multimedia Resources, 2006).

8. See Lois Leffler, *Bible Study Methods: Lutheran Church Women*, part of a report from Lutheran Development for Women, prepared by the Evangelical Church Mekene Yesus in Ethiopia and the Lutheran World Federation, 1973, and *15 Ways to Study the Bible* (Division of Parish Services, Lutheran Church in America, 1982).

9. Dysinger, op cit.

10. Martin Luther, "Preface to the Wittenberg Edition of Luther's German Writings," (1539), 92, 93. For a discussion of this preface, see Ron W. Duty, "Moral Deliberation in a Public Lutheran Church," *Dialog* 45:4 (2006), 349-351, and Robert A. Kelly, "Oratio, Meditatio, Tenatio Faciunt Theologum: Luther's Piety and the Formation of Theologians," *Consensus* 19:1 (1993), 9-27.

11. Martin Luther, 92.

12. Ibid.

13. Ibid.

14. A Lutheran Study Bible will be available from Augsburg Fortress in 2009. Also recommended are the NRSV Harper Study Bible (Grand Rapids, Mich.: Zondervan, 1991) and the New Oxford Annotated Bible (New York: Oxford University Press, 2007).

15, See footnote 3.

16. See concordances such as John R. Kohlenberger III, ed., *Concise Concordance to the New Revised Standard Version* (New York: Oxford University Press, 1995).

17. Kathryn A. Kleinhans, "The Word Made Words: A Lutheran Perspective on the Authority and Use of the Scriptures," *Word & World: Theology for Christian Ministry* 26/4 (Fall 2006): 407, and Martin Luther, "A Brief Instruction on What to Look for and Expect in the Gospels," *Luther's Works*, vol. 35: *Word and Sacrament I* (Philadelphia: Fortress Press, 1960), 119, 121.

18. Martin Luther, "Preface to the Old Testament," *Luther's Works* 35:236.

19. *Luther's Works*, vol. 9: *Lectures on Deuteronomy* (St. Louis: Concordia, 1960), 24.

20. *Luther's Works*, vol. 54: *Table Talk* (Philadelphia: Fortress Press, 1967), 378.

Bible Studies

1. For more information on adult learning, see Malcolm S. Knowles, *The Adult Learner: The Definitive Classic in Adult Education and Human Resource Development* 5th ed. (Houston, Tex.: Gulf, 1998).

2. This is a modified version of a method used by Nancy Boyle and others. For more information on the Relational Bible Study method, contact Faith At Work, Inc., 106 East Broad Street #B, Falls Church, VA 22046-4501 or visit www.faithatwork.com.

Book of Faith Assessment Tools

This final section of the book provides two different assessment tools—one for individuals to use to assess Bible usage, needs, and hopes; and a second designed specifically to encourage group conversation regarding practices and needs of the faith community.

Using "Where Can I Begin?": Individual Assessment

This assessment can be used in various ways to gather information from individuals about Bible usage, needs, and hopes. You have permission to photocopy the assessment tool for individuals to fill out by hand. Individuals may also take this survey online by going to the Book of Faith Web site (www.elca.org/bookoffaith).

Groups of people could take this assessment at the same time together. Be sure to include people of all ages, those who attend worship and/or Bible study regularly and those who do not. You may wish to include people outside this faith community. Consider using the assessment in a conversational interview in person or by telephone or sent out to people in the faith community by mail or e-mail. Or if you have a church Web site, post the survey there and encourage people to take it on line. Results of the assessment, which can be anonymous, can be reviewed by a study group in your faith community, such as a council, task force on education, or a "Book of Faith" group in order to discover needs and plan accordingly.

Using "Where Can We Begin?": Group Assessment/Conversation Tool

The results of this assessment resource can be used to guide conversation in the faith community regarding past and present practices, as well as current needs. It can help the faith community envision a richer engagement with the Bible in the future. Our primary place of encounter with Scripture is communal worship, and although that deserves ongoing conversation, it will not be the focus of this assessment. Because this assessment resource can be used in a variety of settings, including congregations, schools, campus ministries, camps, etc, the term "Faith Community" is used to refer to any of these settings. Responses are primarily for this faith community's insight, wisdom, and growth. An opportunity to share insights beyond this faith community is given at the end.

Use this assessment resource in connection with the Individual Assessment (p. 106) in order to gather a picture from the whole faith community. Discuss the individual responses and use this "Group Conversation" assessment resource in small groups, committees, or council meetings. Be sure to include people of all ages and of differing backgrounds, people new to the community and those here for many years, people deeply involved in activities and those on the edge. Reach out! This assessment resource is designed to be used in any and all groups in the faith community. It could be used all at once, or over a series of sessions, one or two sections at a time. Take time to listen to one another, to remember and affirm, to question and converse, and to dream of new possibilities.

You also have permission to photocopy this assessment tool for individuals or groups to fill out by hand. And this survey is also available online by going to the Book of Faith Web site (www.elca.org/bookoffaith).

Where Can I Begin?
Individual Assessment

Part 1: We Begin by Remembering

1. What memories do you have about reading or not reading the Bible? (Check all that apply.)
- ❏ I remember a parent reading the Bible for himself or herself.
- ❏ I experienced a parent or grandparent reading the Bible to or with me.
- ❏ There was a Bible in our home, but I do not recall people reading it.
- ❏ I heard the Bible in Sunday School and/or Vacation Bible School.
- ❏ I began reading it for myself when I received a Bible of my own.
- ❏ I have negative memories about the Bible.
- ❏ I encountered study of Scripture or Bible study in campus ministry or college religion courses.
- ❏ I have had little or no opportunity to study the Bible.
- ❏ I received a background in Bible through hearing sermons.
- ❏ I studied the Bible in youth confirmation ministry or adult instruction.
- ❏ I remember thinking about the Bible as a book of faith.
- ❏ Other memories: _____

2. *How* do you remember studying the Bible? (Check all that apply)
- ❏ I remember the teacher *reading* the story as we *listened*.
- ❏ I remember pastors/teachers giving *lectures* about the Bible.
- ❏ I remember pastors/teachers leading *discussions* about the Bible.
- ❏ I had *unhelpful* or *unhealthy* encounters with Scripture.
- ❏ I have *no memories* of studying the Bible in a faith community.
- ❏ I remember filling in *workbooks*.
- ❏ I *memorized* verses from the Bible.
- ❏ I remember *singing* biblical verses in songs and hymns.
- ❏ I remember doing *dramatic readings* and *acting* out Bible stories.
- ❏ I remember *watching* Bible stories on TV and/or *using* the computer.
- ❏ I remember *studying* the Bible when I began to teach in Sunday School.
- ❏ I remember _____
  _____
  _____
  _____

3. What memories do you have of someone teaching or preaching the Bible well for you? _____

_____
_____
_____
_____

4. Note two or three basic insights, if any, which were instilled in you from Scripture? _____

_____
_____
_____
_____

5. What words describe your past experience in studying the Bible?

_____
_____
_____
_____

Part 2: Where Am I Now?

1. Do you have a Bible of your own?_____ More than one? _____
What version(s) do you have? (Check all that apply.)
- ❏ New Revised Standard Version (NRSV)
- ❏ Revised Standard Version (RSV)
- ❏ The Good News Bible (TEV)
- ❏ King James Version (KJV) or New King James Version (NKJV)
- ❏ New International Version (NIV)
- ❏ The Jerusalem Bible (JB) or New Jerusalem Bible (NJB)
- ❏ The English Standard Version (ESV)
- ❏ The Message
- ❏ Electronic Version
- ❏ Other Versions:

2. What joys and concerns do you have *about* the Bible? (Check as many as apply)
- ❏ I feel intimidated by Bible study.
- ❏ I enjoy reading the Bible and am strengthened by it.
- ❏ I think the Bible has little relevance for my life today.
- ❏ I believe the Bible is mostly a guide for my moral living.
- ❏ I think the Bible and its interpretation belongs to the faith community, and is not just for private use.

❑ I am troubled by the Bible because of its contents.
❑ I believe it is the pastor who should tell people what the Bible says.
❑ I do not know where to start and how to have a plan for Bible reading.
❑ I study the Bible to learn about God's encounter with humankind.
❑ I believe that studying the Bible leads us to Christ.
❑ The Bible is God's Story and Our Story.
❑ I think that belief in the Bible leads to a prosperous life.
❑ I believe that Christ's incarnation, cross, and resurrection are central in being a community engaging the Scriptures.
❑ I question the reliability of the Bible.
❑ I believe every word in the Bible is factual truth.
❑ I think that every Christian should engage in Bible study in the community.
❑ I believe that through engagement with Scripture people will be strengthened for mission and ministry in daily life.
❑ I believe that Scripture interprets Scripture rather than taking Bible passages in isolation or out of context.
❑ I interpret the Bible in terms of sin and grace (demand and promise).
❑ Other thoughts you have *about* the Bible:

_____
_____
_____

3. How do you *use* the Bible now? (Check all that apply)
❑ In no personal way because I do not own a Bible
❑ In daily Bible reading
❑ As a source of help in time of trouble
❑ To help me realize the human situation and God's unconditional love
❑ For devotions/conversation among friends and/or family
❑ For discussion and growth within my faith community
❑ To challenge me to engage in social justice issues
❑ I attend a Bible study group outside my congregation.
❑ I read a daily devotional book that has some Bible passages.
❑ I follow along when Scripture is read in worship services.
❑ I have a Bible but do not read it very often.
❑ I study the Bible through the Internet.
❑ I regularly dig into Scripture in order to empower my ministry in daily life.
❑ I am confused by interpretations of the Bible that people around me use.
❑ I study the Bible with others to prepare for teaching and/or preaching.
❑ Other responses you wish to give:

_____
_____
_____

4. What sources from the world around you influence the way you think about and interpret the Bible?

❏ Books that I purchased or received from a friend or co-worker
Examples: _____

❏ Radio broadcasts
Examples: _____

❏ Friends and people with whom I spend time each week
What have you learned from them?

❏ Speakers at workshops and synod (conference, etc.) assemblies

❏ Internet, World Wide Web
Examples: _____

❏ Television, movies and DVDs. Examples:

❏ Other? _____

5. What one biblical teaching do you hold as central for your faith today?

_____
_____
_____
_____

Part 3: What Needs Do You Have Regarding the Bible and Its Use?

What would be helpful for your own personal growth? (Check the first column for what you think is needed. Check also the second column if this is something in which you would participate.)

Need	Would Participate	
_____	_____	Help with developing a plan for reading the Bible
_____	_____	Basic skills in reading and understanding the Bible
_____	_____	Further understanding of the various types of biblical literature
_____	_____	More help with Lutheran doctrine in interpreting Scriptures
_____	_____	An advanced course in digging deeper into Scripture
_____	_____	An opportunity to learn more about various ways to teach the Bible
_____	_____	An opportunity to help me connect my biblical faith with daily life
_____	_____	More help and experience in talking about the Bible with others

_____   _____   A time to pray the Scriptures and develop some spiritual
disciplines
_____   _____   An opportunity to teach the Bible to others
_____   _____   A safe environment in which to talk honestly about issues
in the Bible
_____   _____   Other _____

2. What do you think is needed in this faith community and in this church body?
(Check all that apply.)
❏ I want my church to be more clear about how to interpret the Bible.
❏ I believe we need various kinds of opportunities to study the Bible.
❏ I think the number of Bible study opportunities we have now is about right.
❏ I think we need small groups to help people share faith in caring ways.
❏ I think Bible study should begin church meetings.
❏ I think we need more kinds of methods for studying Scripture.
❏ I think we need more Bible study for these age groups:
    ❏ children
    ❏ youth
    ❏ young adults
    ❏ middle and older adults
❏ I think we need training for more people to know how to teach the Bible.

Part 4 : What Do I Envision?

Based on the current situation and on the needs you indicated above, what do you
envision for the future for you and this faith community? What participation and
leadership would you be willing to give? (Check all that apply.)

1. I envision: (Check all that apply.)
❏ People loving Scripture and hungry to hear and read more
❏ People not debilitated but energized for mission and ministry
❏ People enriched and equipped for leadership
❏ Individuals using the Bible more regularly for personal prayer
❏ A worshiping community recognizing the biblical themes in the liturgy
❏ A safe environment where people are not fearful but open to various meanings in a scriptural text
❏ People able to use their biblical knowledge to question, learn, and teach
❏ People sharing biblical stories across generations
❏ A community able to claim and use their Lutheran theology
❏ A community able to fluently speak about its faith in Jesus Christ both within the congregation and to people beyond the congregation.
❏ A consistency and faithfulness in continuing study

2. What participation and leadership would you be willing to give?
- ❏ I would like to join a Bible class.
- ❏ I plan to grow so that I feel more confident reading and interpreting the Bible.
- ❏ I will invite some friends to participate in Bible study.
- ❏ I do not want to be involved in Bible study at this time.
- ❏ I would like to participate in a more advanced course in Bible study.
- ❏ I feel like a beginner and would welcome a class for where I am now.
- ❏ I am willing to teach or team-teach a Bible course.
- ❏ I would like to receive some support/training in teaching the Bible.
- ❏ I would be willing to help initiate/organize Bible studies.

In what setting did you fill out this assessment?
- ❏ At home, by myself
- ❏ With other family members or friends
- ❏ At church with the whole congregation
- ❏ In a Bible study class
- ❏ Other: _____

Your faith community may provide an opportunity to share your personal reflections with the entire community.

Name (Optional) _____

Where Shall We Begin?
Group Assessment/Conversation Tool

We Begin by Remembering

1. What opportunities to study the Bible together were offered in this faith community in past years? (Check all that apply)
   - ❑ Sunday morning classes ❑ for children ❑ youth ❑ adults
   - ❑ Vacation Bible School
   - ❑ Midweek classes ❑ for children ❑ youth ❑ adults
   - ❑ Confirmation ministry and adult instruction using study of the Bible
   - ❑ Midweek gatherings of women and/or men
   - ❑ Long term Bible study series
   - ❑ Specific groups. What groups?
   - ❑ Workplace study
   - ❑ Ecumenical groups
   - ❑ Other _____

2. As a faith community, share experiences of good Bible study, e.g., certain classes, teachers, confirmation ministry, at camp, on retreat, women and men's groups, prayer breakfasts: _____
   _____
   _____
   _____

3. Share with each other challenges or disappointments you have faced as individuals or as a faith community in the past years in regard to the study of the Bible: _____
   _____
   _____

4. Tell stories of how the Bible was used in times of transitions, crises, or celebrations, and what that meant to you: _____
   _____
   _____
   _____

5. Thinking back over the years, what *methods* for studying the Bible were used in this faith community in years past? (Check all that apply)

❏ Teachers *read* the story as we *listened.*
❏ Pastors/teachers led *discussions* about the Bible
❏ Pastors/teachers gave *lectures* about the Bible.
❏ Lay leaders *took turns* leading the *discussion.*
❏ *Few methods* were used because we had very little Bible study at all.
❏ Students filled in *workbooks.*
❏ Students memorized verses from the Bible.
❏ People did *dramatic readings* and *acted* out Bible stories.
❏ People used *media* (film, video, etc) to teach the Bible.
❏ Other memories: _____

6. Think of which of these experiences were unhelpful, boring, disruptive, or discouraging and which were helpful, engaging, and transformative. *Why were they this way?*

_____
_____
_____

7. Over the years what do you recall were the attitudes toward and impressions of the Bible in the life of this faith community?

_____
_____
_____

Where Are We Now?

1. What various versions (including translations and paraphrases) of the Bible do people in your faith community use?

❏ New Revised Standard Version (NRSV)
❏ Revised Standard Version (RSV)
❏ The Good News Bible (TEV)
❏ King James Version (KJV) or New King James Version (NKJV)
❏ New International Version (NIV)
❏ The Jerusalem Bible (JB) or New Jerusalem Bible (NJB)
❏ The English Standard Version (ESV)
❏ The Message
❏ Electronic Version
❏ Other Versions:

Group activity and conversation

For a gathering of the whole or a committee, council, study group, etc., ask people to bring Bibles they own. Put all the versions out on the table and explore the collection. Have people share how they use their Bible. Have them tell stories of when and how they acquired that particular Bible.

2. What opportunities for Bible reading and study does this faith community now offer?
- ❏ Sunday morning classes ❏ for children ❏ youth ❏ adults
- ❏ Vacation Bible School
- ❏ Midweek classes ❏ for children ❏ youth ❏ adults
- ❏ Confirmation ministry and adult instruction using study of the Bible
- ❏ Midweek gatherings of women and/or men
- ❏ Long term Bible study series
- ❏ Classes for specific groups
- ❏ Church Library with Bible study resources
- ❏ Study with the Bible using the Internet
- ❏ "Lay School of Religion" model in the local area, conference, or synod
- ❏ Ecumenical groups
- ❏ Neighborhood or workplace Bible Study outreach
- ❏ Other: _____

3. In addition to the reading of Scripture lessons and the proclamation of the Word in worship, what other *methods* of engagement with the Bible does your faith community currently use? (Check all that apply)
- ❏ *Presentation* of the Bible through story, lecture, film, PowerPoint, etc.
- ❏ *Discussion* of the meaning of Scripture in small groups.
- ❏ *Forums* that begin with *global issues* and topics from *daily life* and move into Scripture study
- ❏ The *telling* of Bible stories
- ❏ Study of Scripture in choir or *worship* planning groups.
- ❏ *Memorization*
- ❏ Use of *art, crafts, music*
- ❏ *Dramatization* of Bible stories
- ❏ Bible Study through *e-mail*, *blog*, or *Web site*
- ❏ Spiritual direction and *praying* the Scriptures
- ❏ Family group Bible reading and *devotions*
- ❏ Pastoral *care* and peer *support* groups reading Scripture together
- ❏ Other: _____

4. What sources (including "secular" and "Christian") influence the way people in this faith community think about and interpret the Bible?
- ❏ Popular Books. Examples:
- ❏ Radio broadcasts. Examples:

❏ Friends, family and coworkers
❏ Television, movies and DVDs. Examples:
❏ Internet/World Wide Web
❏ Other: _____

5. What educational opportunities is this faith community currently offering
those who are already teaching or who are preparing to teach the Bible?
❏ Growth in understanding and interpreting the Bible as a Book of Faith
❏ Growth in Lutheran Theology to open the Scriptures
❏ Growth in understanding stages of faith development through the life cycle
❏ Growth in skill in the use of a variety of Bible study methods
❏ Growth in how to help people connect the Bible with their ministry in daily life
❏ Growth in sharing scriptures with people new to the faith
❏ Growth in how to help people connect Scripture with issues of justice
❏ Growth in use of the Bible in youth and adult catechism classes

6. What is the range of biblical interpretations and beliefs about the Bible that
are present in this faith community? (Check all that are represented.)
❏ The Bible is inerrant and is to be read as literal truth.
❏ The Bible is the Word of God.
❏ The Bible's historical accuracy is questionable in many places.
❏ The Bible is a guide book for moral living.
❏ The Bible tells us interesting and important stories about ancient people.
❏ The Bible is open to multiple interpretations and even contains ambiguities.
❏ The Bible is about the human predicament and God's unconditional love.
❏ The Bible is just a book of interesting stories.
❏ Justification by grace through faith focuses engagement with the Bible.
❏ The Bible is the book of faith of the community, not simply for private use.
❏ Engagement with the Bible through study, prayer, and conversation meets a
deep spiritual hunger and a need for meaning in people's lives.
❏ The Bible can help us be a faith community and the Body of Christ in the world.
❏ Engagement with the Scriptures helps the baptized carry out their vocations
in daily life.
❏ Belief in the Bible leads to a prosperous life.
❏ Christ's incarnation, death, and resurrection are central to engagement with
the Scriptures.
❏ The pastor alone determines the Bible truths.
❏ Scripture interprets Scripture.
❏ People of all ages and backgrounds, including children, can engage the Bible.
❏ The Bible speaks directly about moral issues today.
❏ The Bible predicts current events or events in the future.
❏ The community hears the Bible as law and Gospel.
❏ Studying the Bible as a book of faith equips people for discipleship.
❏ Other interpretations and beliefs about the Bible present in this faith community:

7. The following obstacles to engage with the Bible are found in this faith
community: (Check all that apply.)

❑ Scripture is often taught and read in ways that are confusing or moralistic
or simply boring.

❑ People, especially youth and young adults, have very few positive role
models for significant engagement with Scripture.

❑ Bible study opportunity is offered but people simply won't come.

❑ Reading itself is a challenge for some people.

❑ People who are fundamentalists and literalists seem to be dominating how
the Bible is interpreted and how Bible reading is seen in our society.

❑ People think that the Bible is an ancient text that really has nothing to say to
people's real lives today.

❑ People are suspicious of and/or resistant to invitations to join Bible study.

❑ People hear theological language that they don't understand.

❑ People are just too busy to study the Bible.

❑ All the violence in the Bible is problematic.

❑ People see inconsistencies in the Bible and would like the Bible to give them
simple answers to complex problems.

8. What Bible studies have been led by the pastor(s) in the past two years?

9. What Bible studies have other rostered leaders led in the past two years?

10. What Bible studies have lay people led in the past two years?

11. What does this faith community know about biblical interpretation in other
Christian denominations? How do other churches in the area use the Bible?
Are ecumenical studies offered in this community?

For group conversation

Invite Christians of various denominations to gather to talk about the ways they
use the Bible. Talk about differences or similarities in biblical interpretation within
your faith community and among the various church bodies and where diversity of
interpretations comes from.

12. For further exploration if possible:
What do people in this faith community know about the sacred texts of other
faiths, e.g., the Koran?
For possible conversation:
Invite people of varying religious faiths to gather to share central themes of their
sacred texts. Discuss basic texts that are the center of faith with one another.

What Needs Do We Have?

1. Is there a safe environment for people to talk about their varied, challenging, even contradictory views about what the Bible means? How could it be a place where people are able to be open and honest in asking questions and sharing doubts? What are these places? What is still needed? How can leaders help create such trustworthy places?

2. Are people able to use the Bible as a book of faith to share the Good News of Jesus Christ with members of their families? Their friends? People with whom they spend their week? With a stranger? What would further equip people to be able to do this?

3. Have people in this faith community experienced any of the following in regard to Bible reading and study? (Check any that apply.)
❏ Shyness or discomfort speaking using images, stories, and themes from the Bible to speak about their faith
❏ Feelings of guilt or shame for past inability to read, understand, or study the Bible
❏ Inability or unwillingness to make reading and studying the Bible a priority in their lives
What would help them move beyond these feelings?

4. Are people able to study the Bible in such a way that they are able to relate it to their daily lives and daily ministries? What methods and resources would help them?

5. On a continuum, is this faith community basically energetic or apathetic about their engagement with the Bible?
Apathetic ────────────────────────────→ Energetic
What would help this faith community become more excited about reading and studying the Bible?

6. Are people able to engage the Bible in ways that help them really be inside the texts, to hear, see, smell, and taste what is going on with God and God's people? What would help them engage the texts more fully?

7. Are people studying the Bible together in ways that strengthen and equip them for carrying out God's mission? What is needed to help them do so?

Group conversation: Create an open opportunity to talk in depth about what people believe is the calling of your faith community for mission in the world.
- Some may express the need to share God's grace in Jesus Christ.
- Some may talk about concern for the earth.

- Some may emphasize care for the poor.
- Some may want to be equipped more fully for working for justice and peace.

How does their study of Scripture foster these things and more? What is needed?

8. What is needed so that people in this faith community become more fully equipped to be teachers of the Bible?
❑ We have enough teachers now and they have sufficient teacher training.
❑ We have more teachers than we have people wanting to come to classes.
❑ We need more teachers for
   ❑ young children
   ❑ youth
   ❑ young adults
   ❑ middle and older adults
   ❑ Other groupings. What are they?
❑ Our teachers need ongoing study in Bible and biblical interpretation.
❑ Our teachers need basic education in how to design a class and use various methods of engaging the Bible at various stages of faith formation.
❑ Parents, baptismal sponsors, and grandparents need to be better equipped to share the Bible as a book of faith.
❑ Other needs:

9. How might the pastor(s) role in teaching the Bible be enhanced?

10. What roles can other rostered leaders play in teaching the Bible?

11. How might a conference or cluster of congregations offer ongoing teaching education?

What Do We Envision?

Group conversation: Give each person time to sit quietly and either write or think about dreams they have for the future:

What would this faith community look like if all members were reading the Bible daily and each person was part of a group Bible study on a regular basis? Envision a faith community in which each person had numerous opportunities for Bible study at his or her life stage.

Take time to share those dreams with the group.

1. What would it take to have some of those dreams become reality? Discuss: Why do we want to be engaged with the Bible?

Who will be involved? Who will be leaders?
What gifts do we have among us in this faith community?
What Bible study opportunities do we now have that we should affirm and support?
What new opportunities should we plan to start?
When should we start them?

> Right away?
> After some exploration and planning?
> When and where should they be?
> How will we do this?
> How can we build on the gifts we now have among us in this faith community? What educating and equipping will be necessary?

2. What difficulties do you envision?
- ❏ People will not take the time to come.
- ❏ People will disagree.
- ❏ People will say they will come and start and then will not continue.
- ❏ People will not trust each other enough be able to acknowledge and discuss differences.
- ❏ People will become more divided over social issues based on different interpretations of the Bible.
- ❏ Other: _____

3. Some ideas to respond to challenges and to put your visions into practice: (Be bold!)
A. "There are not enough people coming to our Sunday morning Bible study now."
   Then, start two more. People may need a variety of methods, times, places.
B. "People don't find the Bible relevant to their daily lives."
   Then, go to the places of daily ministry where people are. Walk with them, and listen to them express themselves in the "languages" of their workplace, e.g., "business," "engineering," "coffee shop," "medicine." Start with the questions people ask in the midst of their daily lives.
C. "We need to emphasize evangelism more than education."
   Then, begin a Bible study in the neighborhood. Perhaps work together with ecumenical partners. Reach out to share the Good News and share the Scriptures to help people grow in that Good News.
D. "People would rather spend their time in leisure activities."
   Then, use television, movies, novels, the internet as opportunities for discussion and engagement with biblical themes.
E. "People are so divided over social issues, and it all ends up in disagreement over how we interpret Scripture."
   Then, begin a class on various ways to interpret Scripture. Listen well to each other.

F. "We need Bible study for our youth more than we need it for adults."
Then, start classes for adults. Youth need to see adults questioning, studying and growing in their own faith, digging deeply into Scripture, and becoming strong in their ability to speak about God. Use these growing adults as mentors and guides and teachers of children and youth.

Role-play your own worries and statements of resistance. Role-play your own bold visions of what to do and where to start.

4. Envision specifically some areas on which to concentrate. Check the ones which would be helpful in your faith community. You may want to number them to prioritize your list
   ❑ Neighborhood and workplace
   ❑ Family settings
   ❑ Small groups
   ❑ Faith forums on ethical and justice issues
   ❑ Specific groups, e.g., church council, grief groups, women's groups, men's breakfast, marriage preparation
   ❑ Worship planning to become more aware of Scripture in the liturgy
   ❑ All meetings in the faith community (as a regular part of those meetings)
   ❑ Artistic forms of encountering Scripture (art, music, drama . . .)
   ❑ Congregational or inter-congregation Bible study through e-mail, blog, or Web site
   ❑ Continuing education for more advanced study of Scripture
   ❑ Synod, conference, or cluster events
   ❑ Congregational or multi-congregational teacher education events
   ❑ Other: _____

5. Graced by the Spirit, envision how this faith community might be described five years from now:
   ❑ People loving Scripture and hungry to hear and read more
   ❑ A consistency and faithfulness in continuing study
   ❑ People not debilitated but energized for mission and ministry
   ❑ People enriched and equipped for leadership
   ❑ Individuals using the Bible more regularly for personal prayer
   ❑ People sharing the Bible as a book of faith across generations
   ❑ A safe environment where people are not fearful but open to various meanings in a scriptural text
   ❑ People able to use their biblical knowledge to question, learn, and teach
   ❑ A community able to claim and use their Lutheran theology
   ❑ A community able to fluently speak about its faith in Jesus Christ
   ❑ Other: _____